MEDITATIONS
on EPHESIANS

MEDITATIONS
on EPHESIANS

Leonard T. Wolcott

ABINGDON PRESS   New York Nashville

SET UP, PRINTED, AND BOUND BY THE
PARTHENON PRESS, AT NASHVILLE
TENNESSEE, UNITED STATES OF AMERICA

to her
   who introduced me to prayer
   and to the church
my Mother

FOREWORD

He who wrote this letter was sure of God's design. He wished to convey that assurance to the church everywhere.

From before the beginning of creation, he wrote, God planned to bring us together in Christ. He prepared for us the fellowship of his love. He came to us in Christ. In Christ we turn to him. In Christ, therefore, we come together. Christ is God's expression of his forgiving love. Christ becomes man's expression of his trust in God. God's love in Christ is his evidence of his purpose. Our faith in Christ becomes our participation in God's purpose.

This is the living church. The church provides an experience of unity in Christ. The church, therefore, is to be an instrument to unify mankind in Christ—in God.

This makes quite clear to us why we are here—to be drawn together in fellowship with God and to draw all men to that fellowship. This, if we accept it, gives purpose to our lives and meaning to existence. It colors our relationships. It determines our daily choices.

Nineteen hundred years after the writing of this letter, its convictions speak to our situations. Old cultures have vanished in rapid social change. Old accustomed bulwarks are gone. In disunity and division we have never before so needed unity and peace. But secular society has no center for that unity. It has no clear meaning to give us peace. Our consciences cry out that there must be some universal hope, some enduring purpose. Various movements—nationalist, racist, political, and economic—seek to realize purpose and unity for their followers. But their purposes are limited, and the unity they promise is itself narrowly divisive. The mechanical processes of nature have led to no humanly realized goal. The evolutions of human history apart from God spell no clear meaning. Hope for unity based alone on physically and economically understood social needs is a journey down a dead-end street.

This "Ephesians" letter has a message for today—a message for us. If we read it devotionally we may recover an awareness of God's purpose and of our part in that purpose. We may rediscover the meaning of the church and, through the church, experience the unity in Christ to which he calls us.

The letter was first written in the common Greek familiar to its readers. This translation, as far as possible, seeks to put the ideas of the letter into common English, familiar today. People were very "religious" in those days and they were used to "religious" terms. These terms have lost their meaning for modern "secular" society. Such words as "soul" and "blessing," for example, are not a part of our everyday vocabulary. Yet we today have the same human needs, problems, and responses which people had nineteen hundred years ago. We use new words drawn from sociology and psychology to express these needs, problems, and responses. These words must be invested with Christian meanings just as the religious terms of New Testament days were reconceived by Christian faith. Living Christianity is not concealed in a sacred vocabulary. It uses and transforms the meaning of everyday vocabulary just as it transforms and uses those in the midst of society who accept its Christ.

The purpose of this translation is, through a restricted paraphrasing, to come as close as possible to the intent of the writer in the application of his message to our understanding in our environment.

To the many who, in conversation with me about passages in "Ephesians," shared their thinking, I am grateful. To Carolyn, my wife, for long hours spent as a sounding board to my thoughts, and in typing and proofreading, I am especially grateful.

LEONARD T. WOLCOTT

MEDITATIONS
on EPHESIANS

LETTER TO THE CHURCH

1:1 From—Paul, special messenger of Christ Jesus, sent out by God's will.

To—God's consecrated people who keep faith with him in loyalty to Christ Jesus.

The letter was directed to the early church. The letter is about the church because it is about God's purpose. We read it, and we find it speaking to us and about us who are in the church.

God's purpose called the church into being. As a part of the church we are a part of God's plan.

We are God's people—his consecrated or "holy" people. Holiness does not mean sanctimoniousness. Holiness is the quality of sinners who have come together with love for one another because they have responded to God's love for them. Jesus Christ makes clear how and why we belong to God. It is he who has made God real to us.

He wore no halo. He wore the clothes of a Galilean villager. He mingled with people, and God became real to them. He shared with them the meaning of God. The church is God's people mingling with the world, as Jesus mingled, that God may become real to the world. The church shares with the world the meaning of God.

Paul knew what it was to be sent out by the will of God as Christ's messenger among people. The will of God is God's total purpose of love for mankind in history and beyond it.

To be God's people is to let God fulfill his purpose through us.

Our Father, let us find the fellowship to which thou hast called us, the fellowship of those who are sacred to thee and loyal in the spirit of Jesus. As he was sent to make thee near to men, so set us in the world to make thee clear to all mankind. Amen.

11

A GOOD FELLOWSHIP

1:2 *Grace and peace be yours from God our Father and our master Jesus Christ.*

A letter in Greek-Roman days often began with "greetings and good health."

This letter modifies the usual beginning. Bouyant faith gives old phrases a new sparkling spirit.

"Greetings" becomes "grace": a change in meaning and in spelling of the original word. It means: "May the joy and the inner poise of those secure in their Father's love be yours." "Good health" becomes "peace." It means: "May the wholeness of mind of those who live in harmony with God and so in harmony with one another be yours."

The character of the church the letter envisages is clear: it is a company who live in graciousness with one another. It is a fellowship who sense strong unity among themselves. Their unity is from God and is related to Jesus Christ whom they call their master.

Unlike togetherness of crowds where strangers touch strangers, unlike the oneness of the mob where individual good sense is lost in the hour's passion, unlike the brotherhood of guilds and unions which unite for self-interest, theirs is a unity knit together by the love of God. It is of God from whom alone issues the power of cementing goodwill.

Lead us, O God, to accept thy Fatherhood in our lives. Lead us to accept our brothers and our sisters in thy family. Unite us in the peace of Jesus Christ, our master. Amen.

THE FAMILY OF GOD'S PEOPLE

1:3 *So very good is God, the Father of our master, Jesus Christ, who has done such good things for us through Christ in all that goodness which is vital because it relates us to the eternally best.*

There are words and expressions and looks that are only understood within the family because they grow out of the family's common experience and memories. This letter is to members of the family of God. It is a sharing of the deep gladness that only the family understands.

It reflects the joy with which we look on home when home has proved itself through years of love and security. Home for us is where God is. God is our Father. Christ has brought us to him.

Sheer goodness God gives us. All else called "good" will tarnish. The "good living" which advertisements glow about is based on "much having." Materially based "good living" is like froth that blows away with our breath. It is a false front that falls in the first storm.

Yet there is a goodness that breathes the very breath of life. It is the goodness of himself that God shares with us when we, through Christ, are drawn from our places to his place.

Apart from thee, O God, we are alone. We rattle in the emptiness of things that fade and of time that wastes away. We wander, God, until we find the place of thine abiding, until we stop and rest in consciousness of thee, and look to see where thou dost look and see across the years, and feel and love where thou dost feel and love across the tides of time. Amen.

13

THE PLAN FROM THE BEGINNING

1:4 For, as a matter of fact, before the beginning of the universe he chose us to become, in union with Christ, his own recognized and guilt-free children living in his presence in love.

The letter writer wrote with certainty. God chose us in his plan before our time began. He chose us to be the guilt-free community of his love. Each one of us shares guilt. We all know this, and God knows it. Sin is the life that is lived apart from God. Guilt-consciousness is the longing for our home, for God. When we discover this amazing truth, that God chose us before all time began to be his own, we know we can come back to him. He looks at us, not at our sin. We run to him and cry, "Our Father!" forgetting all the past apart from him. This is what it means to be his "recognized and guilt-free children." These words describe our experience when we live together in his presence.

It is the discovery of self, in a way—the discovery that God is as close and real as the self within each one of us. It is the recognition of what we were made to be and of what, in him, we are.

In Christ this all comes clear. Our God is here! And we are in his presence, chosen, before the universe began, to be his.

As thou hast chosen us, O God, before all time began, so do we now accept thy choice of us. Let thy love rule us. Release us from the sin of self that we may find ourselves in thee. Amen.

A PURPOSE OF GOODWILL

1:5 In love he had already designed for us the relationship with him of children through Jesus Christ. This was in line with the goodwill of his purpose.

Life has meaning.

No meaningless existence with a dead end for us! We have the right to become God's children (John 1:12). We have rich assurance in our destiny. God planned it so. Through aeons of creation, through fluctuating human history, his *goodwill* has been that we should have conscious fellowship with him, as children with their father.

Ours is a family relationship best understood by those who have a strong sense of kinship in a household whose father manages with wise discipline and tender love. A good father is to be honored and obeyed and is ready to give his life to save his children. Such a father we see in God through Jesus Christ.

To be his children is to know he loves us deeply. We are not alone, for we belong to him who is eternal. We are not ours, but we are his who never loses us. Freely we can come to him who has come to us, confide in him, and find his guidance for each day.

The phrase "in love" lies between verses four and five. Translators have been uncertain with which it should connect. In a sense it belongs to both. God's design was made for us in love. To live as his children in his presence is to live in love.

To be his children is to reflect his love in our lives as did Jesus Christ. Because he accepts us as his children, we accept all others as our brothers and our sisters, for they are also his.

We thank thee, Father, for Jesus Christ in whom we see thy love. We thank thee that thou didst design for us a place in the family of God. Bring us from our lonely selves, from separating fears and prejudice, into thy house. Let us live as thy children with thy goodwill for all. Amen.

GRACIOUS LIVING

1:6 Thanks to the reality of his gracious deed with which he has graced our lives, through him in whom he delights!

Pain is real; God's power is more real. Loneliness is real; God's love is more real. Anxiety is real; God's peace is more real. Sorrow is real; God's joy is more real.

Dullness, dimness, darkness of aimless living, hopeless living, and godless living may seem real enough. Greater reality comes in God's gracious deed by which he transfers us to light, to love, to life (Col. 1:13)—that is, to meaning, to fellowship, to wholeness in his presence. This is his gracious deed—it is his gracious gift.

Our life as his children is his gift to us. We do not give ourselves to God. We are his by design. We simply yield ourselves to him to be what he intended from the first. Then we are graced with his graciousness.

Grace is a gift, a favor. It is also power, peace, joy, love, and thanks. To accept our role as God's children is to be gifted with his gift, favored with his favor, powered with his power, harmonized by his harmony, joyous in his joy, living through his love. This is how we thank him for his gift—when our lives reflect his graciousness.

Jesus Christ is he in whom the Father delights. God delights in him as he reflects God's love. Through awareness of Christ we perceive the wide scope of God's graciousness. Our lives realize it as we live for him.

We are grateful, our Father, for the grace of thy goodness all about us, and for the reality of thy being before us. Thou art the real in life, its gladness and its wholeness. We are grateful for Christ who led us to thee. Amen.

AN ACCEPTED PEOPLE

1:7, 8a In him we are released by means of his self-given life—we are forgiven for having failed to live as God intended. This is all in line with the rich goodness of his gracious care which he has lavished upon us.

God created us to fit his plan for unending fellowship.

Yet we ignored him. We assumed existence was made to fulfill our appetites today. We failed to grasp the meaning of history. We dreaded the pain of change and the cessation of self in death. We were lost in the flux of time—in the dark, alone, afraid.

Some of us tried to come to terms with our anxious existence in tepid normalcy, imitating neighbors, or in a monotonous round of activities, or in search for new excitements, feverishly hiding our frustrations.

And yet God offers us the rich fullness of his care. Grace is the word we use to express the marvelous fact that God does for us what we could not do for ourselves. It is his light turned on for us whereby we see in Christ God's plan of goodwill. By this same grace we see how silly, how useless, we have been when wayward from God's plan. By this same grace we see our fellow men for what they really are—objects of God's love and so, potentially and by God's intention, children with us of the Father.

In the light of his grace we come to him. We find release from the prison of our past. We sense the relief a lost child feels when found by his parent. Saved from our frightened past, we go into the future with him. To be with him is to know he has restored us to himself "by his blood"—that is, by his very life. To be with him is to know that our trespasses —our wandering away from him—are forgiven by the very experience of our fellowship with him. His grace is the atmosphere in which dynamic life is lived.

We thank thee, our Father, that thou hast forgiven us for our waywardness from thee, and for enriching our lives each day with thy purpose of love. Lead us, O God, today and in all the tomorrows that follow. Amen.

GOD'S PLAN FOR US

*1:8b, 9 He has even made it possible for us to have aware-
ness and discernment (which we did not have before) into his
purpose. This is in line with his plan which he had already
arranged in Christ.*

When Christ came, many saw in him God's meaning. Christ
has come to many lives—like one who comes to the invalid's
dark room and opens the window and lets in the light, like
one who heals blind eyes and lets them see, like dawn reveal-
ing the path we walk on—where it comes from, where it goes,
and where are the stones to avoid.

A refugee from a totalitarian state said, "I saw many turn
to a false ideology because it came to them with an explanation. It was the first explanation that had ever been given to
them for their misery and of a way out of their misery."

Christ is God's explanation. In Christ we see an unfolding,
universal plan. That plan enfolds all life. When we put
confidence in him, our minds are quickened with perception
into his meaning. They are cleansed of self-frustrating indeci-
sions. We find in him a base for each day's practical choices.

No one can be aware of the plan of God nor understand
the values in existence from the base of a lonely, clamoring
ego. When his love becomes our center, we understand. Then
we live each day toward him and for him.

*God, who set the universe in motion, and yet before and
through it all did plan a plan of love including us, we admit
thee into our lives. Alert us to thy will. Lead us in thy way.
Amen.*

GOD'S PLAN FOR UNITY

1:10 *His plan to bring about the fulfillment of history is to unite under Christ everything in the universe.*

An architect-contractor came to a disordered lot where trees and weeds had been cleared, an excavation dug. Bricks and blocks and lumber, pipes and wires had been left in scattered heaps. But the architect-contractor had a blueprint. He explained it to the workers. They began to visualize just what he saw—a future building into which the scattered bricks and blocks and lumber, pipes and wires would fit.

God has a blueprint. The scattered heaps around us are subject to his plan. His plan requires intelligent response from human creatures because the blueprint is for a household of living love—no house of mere dead bricks.

Christ's appearance in history (Gal. 4:4) made clear the nature of God's plan. Those who, within history, accept the plan will be a part of its fulfillment.

For each of us this signifies that now, in these our days on earth, as we accept the supremacy of Christ, we move toward fulfillment in our lives.

Christ's supremacy is the supremacy of God's love in man. God's love is the persistent conquest of his spirit over hate that separates and fear that would make them insecure. As we serve this love in history, it will serve, through history, to bring God's plan to consummation.

Ruler of history, God, help us to see beyond the horizons of our times and to live above the limits of our tensions. May all our scattered interests, thoughts, and actions be integrated under Christ. And by thy Spirit reconcile us to thy creatures as fellow members of the house of God. Amen.

19

PARTNERS IN GOD'S PURPOSE

1:11 Belonging to Christ, we also have our definite assignment in this plan of his by which he operates everything in line with his resolved purpose.

"Get on board, little children!" sing the words of an old song. The train is going. It has a destination. To go with it, to reach its destination, we must get on board.

God's purpose shall be fulfilled. We "get on board," we move with it, as we share in the outworking of his intent.

God wills the expression of his reconciling love in all relationships. Here is no religion of mere adoration—man adulating God. Here is a religion of operation—God acting through man. Pagans want a God to fulfill their plans for them. Christ's followers have a God who fulfills his plans *through* them. Worship for them is reporting to God and receiving his orders.

The solution of time's problems is found in the resolution of God's will. William Carey understood the gospel when he said, "Expect great things from God; attempt great things for God." When we look in the light of God's purpose at human need, at social problems, at our abilities and possibilities, then we understand what we are called to do, our portion in his plan.

Thou who didst order the universe, order our lives. Forgive our willful dissent from the operation of thy power in history. Show us our part within thy plan. Conform our action to thy will wherever we meet human need for thy reconciling love. Because we belong to thee in Christ, we pray this prayer. Amen.

EVIDENCE

1:12 . . . That we, when we had placed our confidence in Christ, should be evidence of his reality.

The building becomes evidence of the plan.

Many of God's people, like Saul of Tarsus, believed God had a purpose. Jesus described that purpose. He affronted selfish belief that God's purpose fit their narrow schemes. He confronted them with a universal dream, a hope, an assurance, and a demand that they fit God's plan for the reconciliation of all creation. The life and death of Jesus characterized God's purpose. When they put their confidence in this character of God's purpose they became evidence of it. Their lives were a glowing witness of it. They were called, in those days, "people of the Way."

Christ is the character of God's purpose. To believe in that character is to live by it, to fit into God's purpose, to become evidence of his reconciling love.

No society of goodwill is attained by enmity in struggle, and no world of harmony through violence. No godly good comes by evil means. True harmony comes only with persistent practice of love; unity comes only with accepting everyone in Christ's spirit.

To be built into God's plan is to become evidence of the plan and of him who made the plan.

Father, we place our confidence in the Christ-way of thy plan. Humble us from littleness in self to greatness in love until we—our lives—reflect thy glory and become evidence of thy reality. Amen.

IDENTIFIED

1:13 *Belonging to Christ, when you had heard the message of truth, the good news of your liberation, and belonging to Christ, when you had placed your trust in him, **you** also were identified by his promised spirit, his very presence.*

We are identified.

This letter in the Greek repeats the phrases: "In Christ, in him, in whom." The introductory theme of every passage, the basis of every thought, is Christ: "in *him*" who describes God's love, under *his* influence; belonging to *him,* in the atmosphere of *his spirit!*

The message of truth comes to us. We could not search it out. We could not devise it. It comes to us in the midst of existence. At sea a crewman stands all night at the ship's prow or on her flying deck. He listens, looks. What he hears or sees he communicates to the bridge, to the officer of the watch.

To be humanly alive is to listen and to look for meaning. God's message of truth, spelled out in Christ, then comes to our understanding. We direct our lives toward him, and so his message becomes for us good news of liberation—liberation from separateness, selfness, senselessness.

In him, in Christ, we have confidence. We trust the Christly character of God's purpose. He is our direction-finder.

He is our label. Cattle in the unfenced prairie used to bear the brands which indicated their owners. Many Hindus wear on their foreheads the sign of Siva. The only mark or sign Christ's follower shows is the spirit of God in his life. It identifies him with God's people. It is the very presence of God uniting us, investing us with the nature of his love.

Creator and Father, as the nestling bird opens its beak and is fed and the baby opens his arms and is loved, so our hearts open unto thee. Enrich them with thy presence. Surround them with thy spirit. Amen.

DOWN PAYMENT

1:14 His spirit is the first part of our inheritance to come— a receipt for that which is saved up for us, as evidence of his reality.

We take pride in those most dear to us. We want to give and give to those we care for most. We think and speak of their best qualities. In the family of God each and every one is held dear. In such an atmosphere no animosity, nor insecurity, nor distrust dwell.

This is the inheritance saved up for us: the joy of the family of God. United in him, we will live for one another and learn from one another.

Such unity is mankind's dream. Yet without God man has found no more than a forced uniformity where differences are punished or ridiculed. With God, however, we find our Christ-touched differences blend in harmony. We do not lose our individuality, only isolation. Individuality matures in affectionate service to others.

This is no fantasy. It is foretaste. He who faces the sun reflects the sunshine in his face. He who lives by God's spirit reflects God's kingdom in his life. God's uniting spirit is the present experience of our inheritance in him. He redeems our attitudes to others so that we look at them and treat them with God's concern. His love flows through our hearts and washes off the anger and the bitterness. With his spirit we can love the enemy, see beauty in the ugly. As God accepts us, so can we accept our fellow men.

This is living God's tomorrow today. This is the evidence of his reality.

> "Spirit of God, descend upon my heart;
> Wean it from earth; through all its pulses move;
> Stoop to my weakness, mighty as thou art,
> And make me love thee, as I ought to love." Amen.[1]

FAITH AND LOVE

1:15 Because of this, and because I heard of the faith among you who are under the influence of the master, Jesus, and of your love for all who are consecrated to God. . . .

This letter is couched in prayer. It has a double inspiration. It is inspired by God's presence which is a promise and foretaste of what lies ahead for us. It is inspired by the reputation of faith and love among those to whom it is written.

The people of Christ are a congregation that reflects God's future. They reflect God's future in their faith. They are at home with faith. Loyal to Christ, they live in loyalty to each other. Confident in God, they live with confidence in one another.

The people of Christ reflect God's future by their love. Love is the atmosphere of unity God has planned. Years ago Francis Howgill described his congregation: "Our hearts were knit unto the Lord and one unto another in true and fervent love, in the covenant of Life with God . . . in the unity of the Spirit."

Faith and love were the environment Jesus made for others, and his spirit makes for us. It drew the disciples, it draws us, from self-interest to God's concerns. When Christ is among us there is no hiding him. Faith and love make us like a city on a hill (Matt. 5:16).

Dear God, we thank thee for the influence of Jesus. Give us faith to live in the atmosphere he created. Give us love to live with the goodwill he demonstrated. Let him master our thoughts and words and acts. Amen.

24

THANKFUL AND CONCERNED

1:16 I never cease to be thankful for you, and to be thinking of you in my prayers.

The life in Christ is rooted in prayer.

Prayer is not escape from the world. It is bringing our world in thankfulness and solicitude before God. Prayer is the gift of God's spirit, the echo of his will. "Prayer is an offering up of our desires unto God, for things agreeable to his will." [2] His will to unite all involves us in grateful petition for all.

The life of prayer is an ongoing relationship with God and with others. It persists. It is not spasmodic. It does not cease.

The life of faith is a life of thankfulness for others. C. S. Lewis, in *The Great Divorce,* pictures heaven as a place where self-forgetful people gladly accept others, hell as a place where self-centered people resent others.

The life of love is a life of deep interest in others. We are concerned for whom we are thankful. In prayer we confirm them as persons, and we entreat for them as brothers and sisters.

Father, give us the grace of thankfulness for others and persistence in prayer for them. We are grateful for the faith and love of those who belong to thee. With them lead us in thy concern for all mankind. Amen.

FROM AND TO HIM

1:17 . . . That the God of our master, Jesus Christ, the gloriously real Father, may give you a wise and discerning spirit that you may come to know him better.

Radar picks out objects unseen to the naked eye. So, beyond all finite measurements does a wise and discerning spirit, God-given, direct a life's awareness of God.

Knowledge is at hand in the books on our desks. We need to open them, to read them, to study them. The reality of God our Father is by us. We need to turn to him, to look to him, to respond to him. We need not be at loose ends. We can ask for this discerning spirit. The request is never refused. It can be ours if we really want it (Luke 11:13) and if Jesus Christ is master of our lives. He makes himself known to us.

Even without knowing how or why, a son recognizes his father and his father's love. And so can we know God's. He meets our needs and becomes for us a gloriously real Father. "The truly real is valuable and the truly valuable is real." [3] Just "submit yourselves to God," wrote Thomas à Kempis, "and humble your sense to faith, and the light of knowledge shall be given you, in such a degree as shall be profitable and necessary for you."

God of our master, Jesus Christ, our Father, please give to us a wise and discerning spirit that we may come to know thee truly, and so to trust thee surely and to serve thee purely. Amen.

THE DISCOVERY OF HIS PLAN

1:18 ... *That the eyes of your inner mind be illumined to see clearly what is the great expectation to which he calls you and what is the wealth of reality which falls to you in the heritage he provides his people.*

To know God better as Father is to find life's meaning in his purpose. To accept his call is to enter into meaning. The consequence is a richly real heritage. This prayer in Ephesians is for our awakening to meaning and to action.

This letter has a jubilant attitude to life—to life "in Christ." It is like one waking at dawn-light, eager for work, knowing what he does and why, sharing with others the gaiety of God's task, assured of great accomplishment. Morbid anxiety, on the other hand, may circumscribe existence for him who has no motive beyond himself. But here is a new orientation, an eager expectancy in response to God's call.

God calls. We answer. He does not come to do our bidding. We go to him to do his. Of course, if we are closed up in ourselves like a worm in an apple core, we can not hear. We have no hope. When we wing up and out in faith to him, however, hope vibrates through us. This is real. And a realist in the truest sense of the word is he who responds to the "real." "Because the Divine Command is wholly personal and concrete it affects me here and now. The call of God touches me, since it is actual and not an idea." [4]

The ladder of faith which this passage of the Ephesian letter depicts is:

> enlightenment by God's spirit—hearing God's call—
> response with action—fellowship—joy.

A rich, real heritage is found in the action of faith. Meaningful existence in fellowship with God's people is its reward.

O God, open the eyes of our inner consciousness that we may clearly see the great hope to which thou callest us and the rich reality thou dost provide for all thy people. Amen.

HIS POWER

1:19a . . . And how immeasurably vast is his power for those of us who place their confidence in him.

God's force is in action for those who trust in him.

The power of Rome is not mentioned in this letter. Neither are the pressures that can destroy a man's wholeness. Neither would this letter writer have been frightened by sinister totalitarian controls or by shattering changes of modern times.

He was so grandly sure of a greater power, surpassing all man's little might. Therefore he prays, as did Elisha for his servant, that the eyes of people with faith and love be opened to the power of God, that they might know that "those who are with us are more than those who are with them" (II Kings 6:16).

We too can be sure. Empires climb and topple. Demagogues clamber and tumble. "See them clamber, these nimble apes! They clamber over one another, and thus scuffle into the mud and the abyss." [5] Passion burns to ashes; the power of eternal love shall prevail. Fear freezes into oblivion; the force of infinite meaning shall endure. God can make effective the minds he gave us and the bodies he lent us. He alone can fully release the capabilities we have. If we place our confidence in him! If we place our lives at his disposal! To trust him is to walk his way, to write his will into history.

The power is there. A stream sweeps everything in its path as it churns a channel to the sea. It can also turn the millwheel placed in it for productive industry. Divine destiny sweeps away the clutter of human schemes and selfishness. It can also flow through faith and make our lives productive in his plan.

The faith that begins with enlightenment by God's spirit—the conscience alerted to God's purpose—becomes receptive to God's power.

"Be thou my battleshield, sword for the fight;
Be thou my dignity, thou my delight;
Thou my soul's shelter, thou my high tower:
Raise thou me heavenward, power of my power." Amen.[6]

28

HIS PLACE

1:19b, 20 This power is as great as the energy of his conquering strength which he put to work in Christ when he had raised him from the dead and had placed him in the most significant position: along with him who rules all that is of eternal meaning.

Here is the power that can change what seems to be *the end* and lift it to *the ultimate.* It can breathe through death itself to create life undying. It can transform failure to fulfillment. It can make the helpless dynamic. In this letter the writer would arouse his readers to the magnitude of the power available to them—and through them. This power, he writes, took Christ from death and made him the living definition of human destiny.

To describe this power the letter writer uses many descriptive words. It is active power, an inner propulsion. It is conquering power, an outer domination. It is inherent power, prevailing in conflict. Like an inner battery that makes the flashlight's beam or enables the radio's sound! Like rockets that thrust deadweight into space! Like a word, thought, idea that explodes creatively in a human mind! Like these but greater, like God himself who raises Christ from death to his side! This is the power available to work in us.

It is such power that cleared the land and built a hospital in Lambaréné, Africa, and saved the lives of thousands. It is such power that took an oppressed untouchable in India and made him an instrument of hope and helpfulness to his countrymen. It is such power that took a woman in America, crushed to inactivity by crippling disease, and made her a poet of hope and joyousness, an inspiration to millions. It is such power that is available to us—and through us.

If we permit!

O power of God! You raised Christ. Raise us. You drew him to your side. Draw us. In our very weakness be our strength. Use us, as words, in the sentence of your message. Amen.

29

HIS POSITION

1:21, 22a . . . Far above any rule and authority and power and dictatorship and above any person that could be called on —not only in these times, but in times to come. God has arranged everything under Christ.

Christ is the fullest expression of God's purpose; all else is subordinate to him.

Time destroys human plans, but God's purpose, rising above material things, persists through time and beyond it. Change delimits human values, but God's purpose, reigning above intellectual judgment, presides over change and beyond it.

Christ is the fullest realization of our spirits as we subordinate all else to him:

our goals, our judgments, our decisions, our acts to his all-demanding love;

our relationships with human leaders, with earthly authorities, with social controls, with religious ideals.

"One either accepts Jesus as the true revelation of human destiny—which means a radical break with the powers and structures of this world, or one tries to find another absolute authority." [7]

Christ is above all "not only in these times, but in times to come." Our realization in Christ in time becomes a part of God's expression through Christ in eternity. Our today is his; our tomorrows are his. He is our present joy, our future hope. He is more than all earth to us. He is more than all heaven.

O Christ, be ruler over our lives. Be authority in our lives. Be power by which we live. Be discipline in which we live. Be the name by which we test all things. Be the person by whom we judge our deeds of today and our hopes for tomorrow. Amen.

HIS PURPOSE

1:22 He has placed everything under his feet, and he has made him head over everything and he gave him to the church.

Christ is the definition of God's purpose, and his purpose is absolute. Nothing will ever supersede it. Nothing will prevent it. It is absolute because Christ is real. He is the reality of God's personal, purposeful love. Because he is real, only in communion with him can we become real. In him, we become our real, intended selves.

Communion is not mere submission to him who is supreme. It is comradeship with him who commands. We do not do his work for him. We let him do his work with us. This is the meaning of the resurrection and exaltation of Christ. "It is Christ who picks up the threads, Christ who takes the lead, Christ whose presence and power are constant inspiration and strength. The Resurrection means above all just this, that *Christians do not inherit their task from Christ, they share it with him.*" [8]

He is given to the church. He is given to us. Our subjection with all creation under him gives us humility. His sovereignty over all the universe gives us confidence. He destroys our conceit because in judging us he reveals our weakness. He restores our confidence because in re-creating us he reveals his strength. He is the demand given to the assertiveness of our existence. He is the answer given to the question of our lives.

Because, O God, thou hast put us under Christ, we want to be mastered by his spirit. Because, O God, thou hast put Christ over us, we want him, not our opinions, tastes, and wishes, to decide our actions. May we thus truly become the church, a fellowship of people receiving thy gift of Christ. Amen.

THE CHURCH IS HIS BODY

1:23 The church is his body, the completion of him who completes God's meaning in every way.

In our gathering together to him we become the church. The church is his body. So he is given to us who are already his.

Christ completes God's meaning; apart from Christ God is impersonalized—unrelated cogently to the universe. The church also completes Christ's meaning; apart from a worshiping, ministering church Christ is mythologized—unrelated dynamically to society. The church is people gathered from the world to God in devotion, going out to the world with Christ in dedication.

In this church Christ lives permanently. Thus he fulfills us. As helium fills a balloon so that it can soar, our minds can be filled with his teaching, our hearts with his love, our lives with his spirit. We can soar. In this church Christ acts continuously. Thus the church fulfills Christ. "The essential nature of the Church is that so long as the world endures there should be in the world an organism which is truly responsive to the motions and impulses of Christ's mind and heart and will, an organism completely expendable in carrying out his purposes." [9]

We thank thee for Christ, O God, so filled with thee that we through him may understand thy will. May we as thy church be so filled with Christ that the world through us may understand thy love. Amen.

DEAD WRONG

2:1 *And you, you were dead in your wrongdoing and in your misdeeds.*

Remember what you were!

The letter writer reminds us. He says: "Your existence was deadly!"

Our existence *was* deadly, not animated by God's creative spirit. We failed to be what we were intended. We fell over ourselves. We slipped from our ideals. "You know what I'm talking about!" the letter writer implies. Yes, we know.

This is no accusation but a statement of fact. An uninstructed man behind jet-plane controls in flight, without assistance, will crash. How can he avoid it? How can we avoid crash? We try to fly the complicated machinery of ourselves through a world of conflicting traffic. In this secular age, without reference to our creator-pilot, we try. Uninstructed, we get off beam. We crash. We have already crashed.

We failed. We missed the mark.

There is a mark. There is a possibility of success. The mark was set by God. The success is his and never can be ours. Yet we can be part of his success; if we admit our ineptitude and let him take over; if we let him control our lives. This is not blind submission but alert cooperation. We assist his assistance of us.

We confess our failure, O God, to live up to thine intentions for us. We admit the deadliness of self-centered existence. We acknowledge the aliveness of the life to which thou callest us. We come to thee that we may live. Instruct us. Direct us, for the sake of thy love which we have seen in Christ! Amen.

VICTIMS OF OUR TIMES

2:2a . . . Which you were in the habit of doing, following the customs of the times.

You were the victims of your environment.

You existed as others exist. Your faults were their habits—the habits of those who have nothing great to live by. Your failures were their customs—the customs of those who know no God to live for.

Young Saul had seen the pagans with nothing better to do than walk about among the temples of Tarsus. Older Paul had seen them spending their time in the groves of pleasure by the Orontes River near Antioch. He pitied them. Their existence was boxed in. They were unaware of the great sweep of God's plan through history. They did not know what it meant to be God's people.

"You are missing so much in life," said Grandpa to the troubled businessman whose horizons were close to his office. "I'm not aware of missing anything," he replied. The world is not aware of missing anything as it wades through life's shallows. Yet it often feels vaguely sick and silly—going round and round its glittering carousel. It knows that not everything is right in the sweat of clashing interests, the conflict and the clatter.

God is missing. A goal beyond the cry of self and a quest beyond the crash of time are missing. We conducted ourselves by the standards of our times because we knew nothing better. We listened to the patter to which others listened. We looked at the excitement at which others looked. We rushed to resorts where others went. We wanted what they had. We wished to be what they were. We became the slaves of imitation. We were the shuttlecocks of constant activity. We were the prisoners of our pastimes.

O God, we know that we have been missing so much thou hast designed for us. God, we respond now to the yearning of our hearts and minds for thee. Creator of the worlds, be thou director of our lives. Let trust in thee become our habit. Let love for others be our custom. Amen.

IMPERMANENT IDEAS

2:2b . . . Following the lead of the ephemeral ideas of your surroundings, the spirit which at the present time operates among those who have nothing in which to trust.

You accepted the ideas of your times.

In adolescence we may not dare to be different but run in the groove of the gang. In youth we may rebel against the past but conform to the jive and jargon of the present. In adulthood we may settle for the notions we hear around us, on the street, at the lunch counter, bridge club, or cocktail party.

The philosophic climate of many is pagan and paltry. It is a prattle of superficial ideas that press in from every side—from advertisers, popular magazines, "best-seller" books, and from programs entering the home by radio and television. Screen and book stories often reduce ideas to elemental human passions, and religion to sentimentality. News media often narrow the field of attention in the world and oversimplify complex social problems into black-and-white emotional responses, into the paranoia of "for us" and "against us."

We have been influenced by philosophies that underlie the subjects taught in school and college. Useful as they are, most of these ignore God and are ignorant of his overruling purpose in history. Influential as they are, even these philosophies change from generation to generation.

We have been the creatures of our times. This had to be. The challenge of this letter, however, is that we become creatures of God's eternity. Ephemeral ideas operate among those who have nothing in which to trust. Disbelief in God is simply disobedience to the way God has provided for men.

We thank thee, Father, for this world. But we have known its emptiness without thee. We have gone in circles when we have followed its notions, and we have been wasted by its turbulent emotions. Fill us with the spirit of thine eternal way that we may fill thy world with the steady strength of faith. Amen.

CREATURES OF IMPULSE

2:3 *In their company we all once passed our time—yielding to physical desires, carrying out the inclination of human passions and notions; like the rest of them we were just naturally creatures of impulse.*

We were like them. We were like flotsam on the wave of fashion, pawns in the strife of passion; we gave in to desires and excitements. Cut off from keen consciousness of God, our values were upside down. We whirled along on a merry-go-round. Many still exist that way. They get off where they got on: entrance, exist, exit.

We passed our time with them. We were lonely, so we wanted to be where the crowds were to hide our loneliness. We were empty, so we filled ourselves with froth to forget our emptiness. We were afraid, so we built walls around our little groups to exclude the unfamiliar and to hide our fears.

We pleased our tastes with them. Our way of thinking and feeling was molded by our group. We limited our interests to those of our selected neighborhood, our club, our church, or union. We walked about our little cage to and fro. We swam about our little pool like minnows in a puddle. We dared not break out and be different. On those who did we looked as enemies—as a few of his countrymen looked on Jesus.

We were creatures of impulse with them. We laughed with them. We tried hard to have fun. Yet we disdained the very ones who from overindulgence and dissipation fell into disfavor with our group. We were angry with them. It was easy for our indignation to be aroused against anyone or any group that threatened our way of life. Yet we despised those within our group who crossed our self-interest and comfort.

In a crowded world they who live by impulse and by emotion prepare the conditions for regimented society. So ultimately we face the choice of a company controlled by Christ or a civilization straitjacketed by a ruthless human system.

Father, we want to yield to thy discipline, to carry out thy designs, to be moved by thy spirit, to know we are thine. Please lift us from ourselves into thy company. Amen.

GOD LOVES US!

2:4 But God, rich in compassion because of the great love with which he loved us. . . .

But God!

You (vs. 1) and *we* (vs. 3) spoiled God's plan in us. We foiled his purpose for us. We existed in a way that flouted God's rule. We were dead to his intentions. We ignored his actuality.

But *God*—God loved us. Should he not, in disgust, have swept the earth clean of us? He could, in anger, have destroyed us. Our wrongdoing merits punishment. Our deadness deserves burial. But God loved us.

He loves us not because we loved him. We loved ourselves, not him. He loves us not in response to our praise. Our lives dispraised him. He loves us in response to our need —and we need him. He loves us because we are his.

Shakespeare was right:

> The quality of mercy is not strained,
> It droppeth as the gentle rain from heaven.

It comes from an inexhaustible, creative store, the wealth of his compassion.

Compassion is the mark of God. Mary recognized it (Luke 1:54). Zechariah recognized it (Luke 1:72). All recognize it who look to God. We recognize it when we listen to his calling.

Compassion is the movement of God. As water flows into the hollows of the land, so God's compassion flows into the hollows of human emptiness and need. As fire burns down wooden barricades, so God's love burns the barriers away.

God loved us. From before the beginning of time he loved us. God loves us. Now!

May thy love, God, tear away this crust of self in which we die. Our prurience exposed to thy purifying presence, our dry rot breathed on by thy revivifying compassion, our helplessness invigorated by thine arm of mercy, may thy love, God, restore our lives. Amen.

COME ALIVE TOGETHER WITH CHRIST

2:5 . . . Us, who were dead in our wrongdoing, he made alive together with Christ (for remember: it is by his gracious power you are restored).

God loved us. God brought us back to life.

We were dead in wrongdoing. Intended for rightdoing, we ended in wrongdoing. Rightdoing is fulfilling God's purpose. Wrongdoing is failing God's purpose. His purpose leads to life—richly joyous, meaningful life. But we were dead.

God can make alive. He made us alive with Christ. Christ-life is life that looks to God as it moves among men. It is restoration to him for whom we were made. It is going and picking up the prize laid away in the store of his caring. It is using that prize.

So don't be afraid to live. God opened the door. The door is open. Just come through it. Bats prefer darkness. We were made for light. Rats prefer closeness and filth. We were made for openness and cleanness. Come out! Come to! "It is not death a man should fear," said Marcus Aurelius, "but he should fear not beginning to live."

"By his gracious power you are restored." God's safe-conduct is given to us to carry through existence. It is not a *carte blanche*. It is not a promise that we shall be kept from earthly danger, nor that we shall be supplied with every desire. It is the provision of strength to face earthly disaster and of sufficiency for all God desires of us. It is a ticket paid for but also stamped with its destination. New life in Christ is trusting in God's spirit, going his way—with him!

Today, O God, we would live the life thou givest. We would trust the truth thou revealest. We would look to thee, because we want to be led by thee. Amen.

A PLACE WITH CHRIST

2:6 *And he raised us together with Christ and also gave us together with Christ a place supreme with him.*

God made us part of his plan that outlasts all time and over-arches all space.

In Jesus men had seen the meaning of God for human life. In the Crucifixion many had seen the reality of God's love. The letter writer reminds them further of the significance of Christ raised from the dead. Here is a demonstration of the power of love over evil. It works for us, too. We are raised in order that we might live this love's triumph over evil. Jesus was brought to death by religious men because his life threatened the religion of men. Jesus brought God into the midst of life. To be his follower, therefore, means for us that religion can no longer be a pretty veneer. It must mean God brought into the midst of life.

The letter writer also reminds the readers of the supreme place of Christ. The ultimate meaning of God is seen in Christ. And we are raised to that same place of meaning. Supreme meaning possesses us. We need not be troubled in trying to define God. God defines us. God is no longer a projection of our image. We let him make us an expression of his.

Eighty-year-old Pastor Barthulmai spent the evenings in his India village surrounded by neighbors. Most of them were Hindus. Yet in Pastor Barthulmai they sensed God's Christly compassion. He was at home with them not on their level but on God's level of love for them.

Made alive with Christ, we are to live on God's level of self-giving love. His mark is on us. We no longer can pretend to be our own. We no longer represent ourselves. We are his.

We are thine, O Lord. We have heard thy call to new life. We reply to thine invitation. We come to the place thou hast provided for us. But we can do so only as thou dost stretch our minds with thy wisdom and expand our hearts with thy love. Amen.

GOD'S DISPLAY

2:7 . . . So that he might clearly show to the succeeding ages the immeasurable resources of his gracious kindness to us through Christ Jesus.

Through us God shows all ages the magnitude of his love.

He showed it to us through Christ. When we are truly Christ's—when we yield to him—God splendors us with gracious kindness, and *we* become the display of his meaning to the ages.

This is, of course, God's act. We have no goodness of our own to demonstrate. "Good is that which God does, not that which man does." And the good God does outdoes all else in the fluctuating energies of man and nature. God's goodness extends to our human need that we may be the mature persons he intended. Thus we reflect his goodness.

"God Himself, our Father, exceeds all bounds in His generous affection. . . . In the parable of the Prodigal Son the Father runs to meet His child. He puts the ring on his finger and clothes him with the best robe. We too must have this generous nature if we would follow in Christ's footsteps. We must be ready to go to any lengths in humble, loving service." [1]

What he has done for us he can do for others. By what he can do for us the ages of men will see what God can do for them. They know the destructive death that science can bring and the hellish existence that technology can intensify when these practical gifts of God are used without God. They can also see the gladness and calm, the faith and peace, the courage and endurance, the concern and service, of lives that are yielded to God's use. Goodliness without godliness or professional religiousness in place of divine righteousness are sham and mockery. When our lives become pure agencies of God's love, the world knows it is in the presence of the living God.

We are either wholly his, or chaotically ours. Our lives become either witnesses for God or against God. We are either his splendid display or our shabby show.

Father, we thank thee for thy goodness all about us. Employ us as agents of thy gracious kindness. Use us as channels of thy goodwill. Make us displays of thy love. Amen.

RESTORED

2:8a For it is by the power he graciously uses in your behalf that you are restored when you rely on him.

When you rely on him!

No man-made structure binds God to us. No great commonwealth is formed with slogans, no peace achieved by architects of fear; no fellowship is found in sentimental neighborliness, no self-improvement reaches perfection. No saintliness is won by individual effort.

Faith is a response to God that permits his spirit to invade our lives, to pervade our attitudes, our thoughts, until our actions are preconditioned by his saturating influence.

For this God called us. It is for us to answer. God removed the stone from our self-entombment. It is for us to climb out. He has made a way for us. It is for us to walk in it. We need not walk alone. He walks with us.

God's "grace" is his love and power and wisdom directed to us. By his love he cares for us, despite our self-assertiveness. By his power he enables us, despite our weakness. By his wisdom he leads us, despite our ignorance.

God's "grace" is his love and power and wisdom directed through us. "The goodness of man can be no other than letting himself be placed within the activity of God. This is what 'believing' means in the New Testament." [2]

So, "you are restored." You are cured of a diseased ego. You are restored to a continuous condition of well-being in the sight of God. It is the progressive realization of God's purpose. God planned unity. Love makes it possible. Faith accepts it. Restoration, "redemption," is the present experience of goodwill and reconciliation for which God destines his creatures.

Father, how marvelous this is: that thou dost offer us thy love, thy power, and thy wisdom. We would accept thy gracious gift. We would pass this day in reliance on thee and in the gladness of those who are reconciled to thee. Amen.

THE GIFT OF GOD

2:8b, 9 This is not your own doing. It is the gift of God. It did not result from your efforts. You've done nothing to boast about.

It is the gift of God!

When we tried to build castles of our dreams we failed. When we cried to get God's attention cast our way we failed. The castles were for ourselves. The God we called was for ourselves.

Ours is a mad world when people recklessly race after self-gratification and struggle after status in one another's eyes. It ends in madness. Ours is a sad world when people sentimentally fashion a religion to rationalize their prejudice and to justify their pride. It ends in sadness.

It is a glad world when people recognize the love of God and in that love live toward each other. There is no end to such gladness. The experience of being accepted by God and reconciled with one another comes to us from God. We did nothing to achieve it.

God gives. We receive. But we must receive. He comes to us (Rev. 3:20). But we must entertain him when he comes.

We have nothing in ourselves to brag about. When he comes to us we see the sin he sees—the weakness, dirt, disorderedness. We simply open the door to him and in his light see what he sees and say, "Come in."

There is no room for pretense where God is. He comes to stay. He brings wholeness, cleanness, integrity, life. These are his gifts.

We bow our hearts before thee, God. Thou knowest all we are. We cannot pretend to thee. We've nothing to boast of. As we are we come to thee who camest to us. We accept the care, the strength, thou givest us. For all thy gifts we thank thee, but most of all for thee. Amen.

GOD'S WORK

2:10 *God made us what we are: created, in relationship with Christ Jesus, to carry out the good work for which he has provided. Doing his good work is to be the conduct of our lives.*

God made us for great things!

Car manufacturers make cars to carry people, and trucks to haul their loads. Plow makers make plows for plowing. God made us to carry out his goodness. Space engineers design space vehicles for discoveries in space. God designs us for yet greater action in the spheres of his goodness.

We are God's article; we are his deed, done for his work.

We are made for his work; we are not the makers of his work. He who takes a radio kit of wires and resistors, puts them together, soldered and plugged according to a master design, builds an instrument that catches the waves of sound and transforms them into music. Christ Jesus is our master design. We are to be assembled by this design that we may apprehend the will of God and do what Christ would do among our fellow men. Our doing good is fruitless without our being what he would have us be. Our being is frivolous without our doing what he would have us do.

Here is a threefold matter for our prayer: 1. Accept God's creation of ourselves. He made us for his plan. 2. Remember our relationship with Jesus Christ. He is the pattern of God's plan. 3. Seek his guidance to perform his task here and now in the sphere God has provided us. In prayer we look to God that we might know what we are to him—his children. In prayer God points to the world around us that we might do what he would have us do—his work.

This is our life employment, to carry out his goodness. All else is secondary.

God, we admit that our lives are not our own. We are not masters of our destiny. We are thine. We accept the patterns thou hast prepared for us. Give us thy spirit that we may work thy work and effect thy will. Amen.

OUTSIDERS

2:11 Therefore, remember that at one time, due merely to the fact of your physical birth among another people, you were considered outsiders by those who, due merely to the act of a religious rite, considered themselves insiders.

Human self-righteousness separates people from people.

People tend to think their group superior to all others. Such pride supports their group security. This letter writer's fellow Jews claimed superiority through a rite which accredited them, they felt, to God. They looked on non-Jews with contempt. But such conceit is repugnant to God, the Father of all mankind. We still need to beware of this! Lest we allow ourselves to think that the way we practice religion, or the way we state our creed, makes us more acceptable with God! Or lest we religiously rationalize our separation from those whose ancestry differs from ours!

Three points the letter writer makes quite clear.

No human act can make us God's people. Our faith apart from fellowship is foolishness to God. Religiousness that discriminates against others is irreligion before God. Religious practice of a "holier than thou" mood is hypocrisy before God.

No physical fact can prevent us from being God's people. God is no nearer to any branch of the human race than to another, nor to those of any human heritage more than to another. God is one, and in his presence no human divisions remain.

Nevertheless, we are to remember that at one time we *were* outsiders: not by our failure to follow some religious form, nor by the accident of human descent. We were outsiders because we lived apart from God. We followed the crowds who did not know where they went. We flowed with the masses whose only unity was their lack of integrity with God and with each other.

O wind of God, blow down the human fences we have raised. O Christ of God, level the walls we hide behind. In the unbroken plane of faith help us to realize that in thee we belong to one another. Amen.

STRANGERS

2:12 Far from sharing their expectation of the Messiah, you were excluded from the community of Israel. You were strangers to the agreement which carries for them the promise of God's purpose—without a great hope to look forward to, without God in the world.

Human self-centeredness separates people from God.

The letter writer described the condition of those who lived apart from, and unaware of, the Jewish heritage of hope. His description fits as well the secular society in which we live. We *were* outsiders.

First: We did not understand that God can touch our human lives and draw us to his great consummation. We lived for our own ends and not for Christ.

Second: We did not experience the bond of those who know they are God's people. We felt uncomfortable at thoughts and conversation that referred to God and to God's concerns.

Third: We were foreigners to God's kingdom. We were not familiar with the vocabulary of faith. Churchmen sometimes speak of God's people as "covenant people" (or people of the "agreement"). By this they refer to those who consciously take part together in fulfilling God's plan. As "outsiders," apart from God, we found no meaning in such an idea.

Fourth: We had no great hope to live by. We bought existence on time, as it were, plagued today by bills and repairs for yesterday's pleasures.

Fifth: We did not know God. We existed as though God did not live. Worse than "atheists" who denied our substitute faith and ridiculed our imitation god, we were *God*less in our day-to-day world.

God, our Father, save us from God-less religion and from hopeless existence. Draw us to thy purpose. Company us with thy people. Refresh us with thy hope for tomorrow and thy Christly presence for today. Amen.

FELLOWSHIP WITH A FOCUS

2:13 *But **now**, associated with the Messiah Jesus, **you** who used to be remote from us have become close to us. We are centered together by Christ's act—his self-given life for us.*

Christ-centeredness brings people close to one another.

The emphasis is Christ Jesus. When we see the meaning of his sacrifice, his death—when we see in him the magnitude of God's love for us—we draw toward him and find ourselves drawn toward others. The fact of our faith is a response to the act of his love. We are brought together with Christ, together with one another, together with ourselves.

The *now* of Christ replaces the *then* of self. In Christ our lives become centered. In self they were scattered. In self-centeredness we diverged from one another. In Christ-centeredness we converge with one another. Hell has been described as the ultimate in isolation, heaven as the ultimate in fellowship.

Then we were so far from Christ we did not understand what he was; we did not care what others were. We were outside the house of faith. But *now* we've been brought inside. We understand what Christ is. We care what others are. *Then* we were remote from one another. Those far from us were not important to us. *Now* we understand what the ancient man of God realized—that the far away and the near are equal in God's care (Isa. 57:19). Christ has changed our attitudes and relationships. Those who are far away—whether on the other side of the world, or strangers in the next apartment, or opponents to our social views—are as important to us now as are those who are near and dear.

We are close to one another when we are close to Christ. He is our focus. The life he gave up for us is the life we take up for him.

God of Christ, triumph over our insolent self-love. Drawn to thee, may we find each other in thee. Amen.

BROUGHT TOGETHER IN CHRIST

2:14 *For it is he who brings us together, he who made our two groups one, who broke the barriers down that separated us, which had made us hostile to one another.*

Christ is the definition of our peace. His spirit binds us.

We set barriers up. Our barriers we built of self-interest, self-concern, disregard of others. We built them round a group to which we could belong—to defend what our group had gained—to block intruders out. We made their differences excuse for separation. We fenced them out and thereby fenced ourselves in. We cut them off and thereby cut ourselves back from a full life. We excluded others and so excluded God. To include him would be to include those whom he includes. And he, in love, includes all.

Christ tore the barriers down. Barriers do not make for peace. Among the nations, when treaties are made but distrust remains, there is no peace. Peace with armaments is not peace but truce. Among neighbors, when legal barriers go but prejudice remains, there is no peace. Indifference to others is not peace but toleration. We tolerate others but our inner attitudes remain intolerable.

Christ means unity and not mere parity. This letter writer was not speaking of equality before God of Jew and Gentile (or of African and Asian, or of Negro and white). He wrote of unity where separations disappear. In our new relationship with Christ we become as one.

Thank God, in Christ the fences fell. We all belong to him who is universal love.

O Universal Love, weed from our minds all prejudice and from our hearts all fear. Tear down the walls we've built that separate us from thee and thine. O Father of mankind, let us be joined to thy purpose of peace. Amen.

A UNITED HUMANITY

2:15 He, by the very nature of his life on earth, did away with an order of relationships based on rules and regulations so that he might create, through our personal relatedness to himself, a united new humanity. This is the way he brings about peace.

Our peace is in union with Christ.

It was the aim of Jesus to help men find deeper foundations than rules and regulations for their relationships. This aim underlies the Sermon on the Mount and underlies his very conversations with religious leaders of his country.

In an ordered society rules may be contracts between potential enemies; regulations may be controls over possible anarchists. Through the generations wise teachers have tried to fashion good rules for human behavior. Able statesmen have tried to implement good regulations for social concord. But

> Those who put their faith in worldly order
> Not controlled by the order of God,
> In confident ignorance, but arrest disorder.[3]

Sturdier than rules, an inner impulse of goodwill is what Jesus called for. Stronger than regulations, inner control by God's spirit is what Jesus showed. How miserably current schemes collapse which, denying God, think to build a new united humanity by regimentation. How fragile our fellowship that fails if, confessing God, we maintain a kind of togetherness simply by evading Christ's demands, by disregarding vital differences among us. Loyalty to Christ does not disregard our differences but surmounts them. Linked to him, we are not melted down but rather we are, each individual bit, fitted, framed together, in his plan. This is God's new creation.

This is the peace God brings about.

Maker of our peace, control our lives by love. Teach us the unity of respect for each other. Bring us, through loyalty to the way of Christ, into the new humanity which is our destiny and our only hope. Amen.

RECONCILED

*2:16 He did this by way of the cross that he might recon-
cile both groups as one body, joined to God, having brought
our hostility to an end in himself.*

We are the church of the reconciled.

We are reconciled by the cross: by God's act in Christ.
Without the cross we live by an uneasy treaty; we respect
that we might be respected; we do good that good be done to
us. But on the cross Jesus surrendered his right to live rather
than surrender God's right to love. When we accept the meaning of the cross in our lives we accept the right to live above
ourselves. We surrender our little, limited desires and give
to God his right to love through us. This joins us to God.
This joins us to all who are joined to God.

Village Balpur in India was divided by bitter quarreling. A
teacher settled among the villagers and told them the story
and meaning of the cross. They yielded themselves to Christ.
They were reconciled. They put the message of Christ, their
peace, in verse and sang it to an old folk tune. Then, as one
body, through the fields and towns they marched to an Easter
celebration. As they walked they sang their song. They were
one body now—pilgrims, witnessing as they went to reconciliation in Christ.

"The church is, by its nature, a body on pilgrimage." [4] On
pilgrimage it witnesses and puts in practice, as no human in-
stitution can, the ideal of inclusive fellowship. It does when
it *is* the church under the cross, joined to God.

For Christ absorbs our hostilities in love.

*Father, Father of Christ Jesus, we yield to thy love. We sur-
render our hurt egos, our strong desires, the perplexities of our
misunderstanding struggles. We yield to thee the right to love
through us, to make us one body joined to thee. Amen.*

PEACE

2:17 For when he came among us he brought the glad message of peace to those of you who were far off and peace to those who were near by.

It is his peace he brought us.

Christ is no ideal in a distant blue yonder. He came among us. Some of us have been far off. Like the prodigal son we lost ourselves in distant places. Far from home, from our ideals, far from ourselves!

Christ came and brought the message of God's peace. He identified himself with men in the spirit of love. He was crucified for men in the service of love.

No matter how far we are separated by distance, or by interest and opinions, or by customs and culture, Christ speaks to the conscience of every man. When we accept him, we find ourselves accepting one another—diverse yet divinely united; individuals, yet in company; at peace with God, and so at peace with others; as Charles Lamb said, "a unit in aggregate; a simple in composite."

His peace remains. Some high moments of shared faith or of crisis may bring a momentary sense of fellowship—a pause in our separated striving with others. Christ brings *peace,* not a pause. Peace; a steady, disciplined peace that remains!

His peace constrains. Jesus said of the world's kind of peace: "I came not to bring peace, but a sword." Yet he also said, "My peace I give to you." His peace led the disciples to persecution, suffering, death. Yet it was peace because it was in company with God, it was in love for fellow men. It is peace because it compels us in harmony with God's will and frees us from frustration.

Father, give us this peace, that we may in Christ's spirit, be identified with our fellow men and in Christ's love be crucified for our fellow men. Father, give us this joy. Amen.

TO THE FATHER

2:18 Because it is through him that we, both from far off and from near by, united in the same spirit, have access to the presence of the Father.

We come together to God; we come in the spirit of Christ.

We come together to God. God does not belong to our separated egos. He is not hidden in our way of life, nor bidden by our opinions. We have to leave our self-protected paths to go to him. Going to him we find our brothers.

Through Christ our roads join. All our different roads join under the same arch—his spirit. What is his spirit? Look at Jesus Christ! In him we see the actualizing of God's spirit. If God were not like Christ, we could go our different ways to our different images of God. But because God is like Christ, we come together in his same spirit of self-givingness, of forbearance, of goodwill, of assurance and compassion, of new creation and purpose.

Through Christ we understand that we are children of our Father. As children of our Father we understand that we belong to our brothers in him. To delight in the wonder and presence of God and to discover that persons near by and persons far away also delight in his wonder and presence is to discover the warmth of unity. We are together in the presence of our Father.

> To walk together to the kirk,
> And all together pray,
> While each to his great Father bends,
> Old men, and babes, and loving friends,
> And youths and maidens gay! [5]

Father, it is good to come to thee and in thy presence find relief from anxiety for ourselves and from antagonism to others. Keep us throughout the world united in thy spirit. Amen.

THE FAMILY OF GOD

2:19 Now, therefore, no longer are you foreigners and strangers away from home, but you are fellow citizens with God's consecrated people, family members at home with God.

We are members of the family of God.

Before, we were not. We were foreigners who did not belong. We were strangers away from home. But now—

Now we are fellow citizens with God's people. God's people are they in whom God plies—in history—his power, wisdom, and love.

Before, we were, perhaps, houseguests with God's people and went to church and worship. Yet we were more at home in the pursuits and passions of the world. We were, maybe, neighbors to the family of God and even served the church for all the good it does. But we were not kin. We knew no close-binding spirit with God's people. We were not comfortable in God's presence. But now—

Now we are full members of the family. We've come indoors. We've found a place already set for us with all God's family. We have the rights of God's children and the responsibilities as well.

Only in the fellowship of love is the church Christ's church, and only then does God's kingdom come. Only when we are at home with God! So, let us no longer be tentative about God. We are each one his child among his children. Listen to him!

We thank thee, God, that we can be at home with thee. We will no longer take, irresponsibly, benefits as foreigners in thy city or as guests within thy house. We will accept thy love, Father, and we will obey thy will. Teach us by Christ's spirit. Help us for we are thine. Amen.

THE HOUSE OF GOD

2:20 *This house is built on foundations laid with those who have been God's spokesmen and with those who have been his envoys. The corner foundation stone is Christ Jesus himself.*

God's house is built of people.

It is very real. It has to do with us, on earth, in time. It is built to last, however. The Bible, for example, is a record of men's human experiences—like ours, but touched by faith in God. So God builds his house with people set into its lasting structure.

Its foundations were laid with people who were God's spokesmen. These were people who questioned the problems of life that human beings face. They questioned in faith and they heard God's answers and they spoke those answers to the world. We hear God's word to echo it.

Its foundations were laid with people who were God's envoys. These were people whose lives were touched by Christ's. When he saved them from themselves he sent them out to others. They discerned in his calling a task to which they were designated. We are touched by Christ's spirit to share it.

The corner foundation stone is Christ. In him the generations have seen God's word among the people. His teachings were for people in people's relationships. His message was about God's rule among people. The foundations and walls of God's house are squared from this cornerstone. Our home is measured by the meaning of Jesus Christ. Our persons, our acts, our lives are, also.

God's house is built for people.

O God, we thank thee for the firm foundation of thy house. Like the lives of thy people who were before our times, may our lives speak for thee and our acts witness to thee. We take Christ Jesus for our measure. Amen.

GOD'S TEMPLE

2:21 About this corner foundation stone the entire struc-
ture is fitted and grows into a sanctuary sacred in its relation-
ship to the Master.

God's people are built into his sanctuary.

As they grow together in faith and fellowship, among them
the presence of God becomes evident.

The reason is Christ. Through every passage of this letter
the theme repeats, the reminder comes: "in him"; "in whom";
"in Christ." Joined to, related to, Christ all this unity comes
about. Like the parts of wood and stone and brick that make
a building, God's people fit together. They must be made to
fit together—all joined to Christ and in him joined to each
other. Sometimes this fitting requires the plane, the nail, the
mortar, the adjustment until they fit. And when they fit
they add to the building.

God's people are living human parts of a living divine structure. This means that to be fitted in it is to become conscious
parts of God's purpose in this life. It means to yield ourselves
to him who knows where each best fits his plan.

The day will arrive—now may be here—when we shall know
and the world will see that we have become the temple where
God dwells.

Here, O God, we are. Our abilities and our limitations are in
thy hands. Mold us to thy plan. Fit us together in the frame-
work of thy will. Use us to make a sanctuary where all the
world can come to worship thee and to know thy meaning.
Amen.

GOD'S DWELLING PLACE

2:22 Joined to him, you also are built into the structure along with others as a place for God to inhabit.

We become God's house. How can this be?

This can be as we join ourselves to Christ, to him who made God personally evident in human life, and by whom we are made sensitive to God's being—to his presence and his purpose. It can be as we live under the influence of his spirit.

God the builder builds his house. God builds; we are the built. The worth of man is found as he becomes a part of the work of God. Without God man throws his life away in worthlessness. All human systems that discard God and regard man end up by discarding man the individual as well, because apart from God he has no dignity. Apart from God he is anxious breath exhaled in emptiness.

The value of the house of God validates us who are a part of it. Our worth is not our own but God's, and so it endures forever. He lives in us when we, together, as an affectionate family, are ready to make our fellowship a witness in the world. He lives in our witness.

When? Now! For God is always fully here. Thoreau said, "God himself culminates in the present moment, and will never be more divine in all the lapse of the ages."

O God, our Father, dost thou dwell in us? We know thou dwellest not in houses we make for thee. So take us and make us into thy house. We lay down our weapons of anger, we give up our tools of ambition. What we are, as we are, take, remake. We thank thee that we can be part of thy house. Amen.

BOUND TO CHRIST

3:1 *This is the reason that I, Paul, am a prisoner of Christ Jesus in your behalf—you people of the nations.*

We are captive to Christ for the sake of others.

Paul had found his place in God's plan. He had been built into the structure of God's temple, fitted, bound to Christ, the foundation stone. His existence had meaning for others now in the total meaning of God. Prisoner to the Roman government? That was incidental to Christ's control of his life.

No one is completely free. We are bound to one another. In our human relationships we sin against one another when we use others for ourselves. Much of our vaunted personal freedom is a violation of one another. We violate others for ourselves when our emphasis is on comfort rather than courtesy, on convenience rather than courage. Courtesy and courage are measures of self-mastery that free us from ourselves.

Yet we are most free when bound by the masterful purpose of Christ. Dependent on Christ, we no longer center our attention on ourselves. We become attentive to others.

"Friend," said the Spirit to a miserable visitor from hell, "could you, only for a moment, fix your mind on something not yourself?" [1] Never pitiful is attentiveness to others. Never pitiful is the Cross that suffers with and for those that suffer, and longs for those who are lonely.

A prisoner of Christ can be nowhere except where Christ would have him.

"Make me a captive, Lord, and then I shall be free;
Force me to render up my sword, and I shall conqueror be.
I sink in life's alarms when by myself I stand;
Imprison me within thine arms, and strong shall be my hand." [2]

COMMISSIONED TO SHARE GOD'S
GRACIOUS LOVE

3:2 You must have heard of my commission to bring to you an awareness of the love, power, and wisdom God has for you.

"God has given me a responsibility in his household to share his goodness with you."

This the letter writer reminds his readers. To be bound to Christ is to bear a responsibility from God to others. It is to share the generosity of God with others. It is to go any length in loving service to others.

God calls us to come to him that he might appoint us to be stewards—distributors—of his grace. "Grace" is the word used for God's love, power, and wisdom directed to and for man. It is God's gift. Usually it is thought of as God's goodness to us. Here, it is spoken of as God's enabling us to share his goodness with others.

What is received is to be shared. What flows in is to flow out. What is learned is to be taught. The baby receives the family's love. As he grows, he learns to give as well as to receive. As the child matures, he learns to share in the co-operation of love and in the obedience and judgment of love. As we grow in the household of God, we mature as stewards of God's gracious love to others. If not, we are social idiots in the church and not full members of God's family.

Father, help us, as we look to thee, to grow in awareness of thy love and power and wisdom. We accept the responsibility which thou dost give us. By thy spirit let us love and serve others, this day, as Jesus would. Amen.

PAY ATTENTION

3:3 I have already written to you briefly about the disclosure by which the hidden meaning was explained to me.

The deeper meaning of life and its purpose is understood by those whose attention is on God.

Attention unlocks what seems secret. Lack of faith has its roots in lack of attention to God, to the sources and significance of life. A lawyer despaired of meaning in his world, yet he wanted it to have meaning. He rejected faith because, he said, it gave no clear answers. But when he concentrated attention on the kind of God Christ portrayed, and applied that picture of God to the pieces of life about him, he discovered meaning.

Christ is a definition of God, bigger than our minds. That is why religion is unimportant that wishes to confine Christ in a definition, and trivial when it tries to entomb him in a shrine. That is why Christ is big enough to be the corridor of life where we can meet God and go with him. He is "the one great supreme link between man and God as at once the essence of divine nature and the ideal of all human nature." [3]

Christ is God's listening to our human need. Christ is our listening to the will of God. In Christ we know God understands us. In Christ we understand what God wants us to know.

Aware of the world about us and at the same time attentive to God, we become sensitive to his spirit. What had been the mystery of the unknown in a meaningless world becomes God's eternal will related to man's time. The hiddenness of faith becomes disclosed in the openness of life lived to and by him.

"I ask no dream, no prophet ecstacies,
  No sudden rending of the veil of clay,
  No angel visitant, no opening skies;
  But take the dimness of my soul away." [4]

NOW WE CAN UNDERSTAND

3:4 By reading what I have written, you will understand my insight into the deeper meaning of Christ.

We too can understand the deeper meaning of Christ.

We are helped in our understanding by reading the record of those who have kept their attention on Christ. God is made clear in Christ, and Christ is made plain through those who apply his meaning to life.

Meaning does not come simply in a formula of words. Deeper than words, for example, is the meaning of friendship. And friendship often is a bond that makes the difference between loneliness and assurance, between despair and hope.

Deeper than words is the meaning of Christ that touches a man and anchors him to all that is real. A meaningful life is more important than precision of religious definition. In *The Robe* Lloyd Douglas described the way Marcellus, after having seen the crucifixion of Jesus, would stop in a conversation and ask: "Were you . . . out . . . there?" Out there something remarkable had happened that no one could forget. It gave Marcellus meaning and direction. It wiped out selfish, senseless existence. Something potent, something genuine took place. A mystery? Yet plainer than words! It did affect men and still affects men plainly, deeply.

> A sense sublime
> Of something far more deeply interfused,
> Whose dwelling is the light of setting suns,
> And the round ocean and the living air,
> And the blue sky, and in the mind of man;
> A motion and a spirit, that impels
> All thinking things, all objects of all thought.[5]

This perception, God, that has come to those who have turned their thoughts to thee, who have responded to thy spirit—let it come to us. Let us perceive the deeper meaning thou hast for our lives. Amen.

INSIGHTS COME

3:5 . . . Which was not made known to people of other generations as it is now disclosed by his spirit to his own messengers and spokesmen who are consecrated to him.

Insights into the meaning of Christ come to those whose lives are directed in his service and projected for his witness.

When you turn on the radio and hear a jumble of confusing sounds, you adjust the dial until you are attuned to the frequency you want. Stabilizing knowledge, poised and meaningful purpose, come when our lives are dialed and fixed to the clear channel of God's spirit.

The writer of this letter sees time moving toward God's fulfilled plan. There is a difference between the former "then" and the present "now." *Then* the generations did not know or understand the meaning of God's plan. But *now* we can understand. *Now* stands at the threshold of *will be*. We are citizens of God's tomorrow.

Yet many still live in yesterday. In a heritage enriched by the influence of Christ they live in ignorance of his deeper meaning for their lives. Thomas à Kempis said, "The whole man doth slide off into external things."

On the other hand, "The more fully one understands the Christian gospel, the less his mind is prey to the newspapers, the radio, and the conversations he hears around him." [6] Insight into Christ's deeper meaning clears the mind of the confusion about us. This happens as our lives are consecrated to him, dominated by his spirit.

Then we become messengers of his deeper meaning and spokesmen for its application to every area of life.

Our Father, we thank thee for thy messengers who have brought thy meaning to our attention and for thy spokesmen who have applied it to all of life. We accept thy meaning for us. Teach us to wait in quietness and willingness to know thy will. Amen.

SHARED INHERITANCE

3:6 . . . That the people of the nations might inherit with us, and share with us, as one people, and participate with us in the promise proclaimed through Christ Jesus.

God's plan is for fellowship.

Christ focuses that fellowship. Christ attracts us into one body. The mouth cannot speak without the breath in the lungs. Muscles cannot absorb energy without the stomach. No one can live to himself. No one can live fully who restricts his interests, activities, and concerns to a limited group.

Christ draws us into one family. There is no family life apart from the members of the family. There is no social completeness apart from love for one another in the love that God, the Father, gives.

Jesus Christ is God's invitation to us into his fellowship. Jesus Christ makes clear to us the nature of God as God relates to man. He makes clear that God's rule in our lives is his goodwill among us.

Jesus Christ is God's summons to us. The summons comes with love because it comes from love. God is love. His summons is to love. He who will not lose himself in love maintains a lonely isolation through the years of his existence.

"The people of the nations" have had limited togetherness in separate groups. Their loyalties to tribe, class, or nation divide them from one another. The gospel is good news for them: the offered heritage of oneness in Christ. In him a new loyalty to God—and in this loyalty, loyalty to one another—supersedes all separating loyalties. Only that which is higher than self and than any temporal, finite center can draw men into enduring fellowship.

The promised plan of God is one in which there is full sharing of all we have, full giving of all we are. It is laughter together and suffering together. There is no harmony in the solo. There is no rainbow in the single color.

Father, we are grateful for thine invitation and thy summons to thy fellowship of love. We would participate with all thy people in thy promised unity. Amen.

THE PRIVILEGE TO SERVE

3:7 I have become a servant of this good news. For this task God's gracious gift is given to me, his strength is at work in me.

In the fulfillment of God's plan we serve his love to one another.

The letter writer is saying: "God's good news masters me, it drives me with its grace and energy."

A pen is made for writing—supplied with nib and ink for writing. Yet, by itself it does not write. A hand moves it across the page. With it a writer writes what he would say.

God would say great words in human history. We were made to write his will across the page of time. We cannot write for him or without him. Yielded to him, we write. He fills us with his love and wisdom. His strength flows through us.

We do not, with our flagging energies, serve our fellow men in order to please God. We serve him, and he gives us love with which to love. The word (in the Greek) "to serve," "to minister," may come from the root "to run after." We follow him. We wait on him. Thus we are ready at his bidding to carry his message, to do his task. His strength enables us.

Since God's plan masters us, what great things he can do through us! The more we wait on God, attentive to his will, the better he can use us as agents of his design.

We wait for thee, O God. Set thine eternal purpose in our hearts. Untrammeled with ourselves, may we be filled with thy love. Put us to tasks too hard for us that we may draw upon thy strength. Amen.

THE WONDER TO TELL

3:8 *Even to me, less than the least of all God's people—to me was given this privilege joyfully to proclaim to the people of the nations the untrackable riches of the Messiah.*

We tell about the riches of God. We cannot help but tell. It is a daily wonder we cannot contain or keep to ourselves.

This joy drove the apostles—those who had been with Jesus. It drove Paul to bring to nations a heretofore unimaginable piece of good news. The letter writer is astonished at so great a privilege: that it should be given to him to share the good news of "God-come-to-us to take us into his plan."

This privilege is given to us as well. We are not important in or of ourselves. God's gracious love is tremendously important to us. It makes life eternally meaningful. Accepted love becomes a compulsion to share its wonder with everyone. A farmer drops a seed into the soil. The seed dies as a plant grows out of it. An electrician drops some solder with a soldering gun. The solder, melted, binds a wire transmission for great power.

God privileges us. In our self-importance we have our hands too full of self to receive God's gift. But in our humility, as we die to self, melted down, he uses us. This is his gift—to use us for his purpose.

It is a privilege to share his secret with the world. It is a rare responsibility. The secret is where his treasure is stored. There is no end of this treasure. There is no limitation to it. No formula can define it. No organization can confine it. Secular human agencies have sought to imitate the compassion of Christ. It cannot be copied. It cannot successfully be counterfeited. It can only be accepted, this treasure, and then spent.

Christ is our wealth. (Christ, the "Messiah," is the coming of God to us.) When this wealth is found in us, God spends us as purses of his generosity.

Enrich our poverty, God, with thy wealth of love. Enable our weakness with thy power of love. Spend us for thy purpose of love. Proclaim through us the joyful news of thy love to all the nations. Amen.

A SECRET TO SHARE

3:9 God, who created all things, has always had a secret purpose for his creatures. It has always been obscure to men, however, through their lack of comprehension of the meaning of God. To make God's arrangement clear to all men: this is my privilege.

Perhaps we were going in circles, but now we see the way.

Lost in mountain jungles a group of hikers met a man who knew the way. He had explored these hills for years. He took them to a mountaintop clearing. He pointed out the way they had come and the road that led home. From the hilltop they could see.

Brought to the place of God in life, we see. We understand his arrangement. We are to follow in his way. Life's meaning was hidden to us because we did not know God. God in life is like the turning on of x ray whereby we see inside what had been opaque. What God displays to our understanding is his plan—and the confusion of our own.

God created with a purpose. His creatures are to share in the fulfillment of God's plan. Their deviations do not deter this plan. They frustrate only their part within the plan.

The letter writer's privilege was to make God's purpose clear to all. This is our responsibility. In well-regulated homes children have duties. As they participate in household arrangements they become more a part of the family. They grow as reliable partners in the home. Our right to be God's children is our acceptance of responsibilities in his household plan. We receive responsibilities from God. We hold them for others. We make God's arrangements clear. We do so when we treat all men as brothers, all women as sisters. We do so when we share the world's goods and share the chance for self-expression in every life. We do so as we extend persistently the fellowship of God for all his creatures.

This is our privilege.

For the right to be thy children, Father, we thank thee. For the responsiblity to be servants of thy purpose, God, we praise thee. Amen.

PLAN OF WISDOM

3:10 That through the church the infinitely varied wisdom of God might now be made known to those in places of highest rule and authority!

We, the church, are now the guides. We are to point all to the way of God.

The unworthiness we feel to bear God's message (3:8) combines with undoubting confidence in making known his wisdom to the world. Any church group with an inferiority complex or false modesty or fear before the wisdom of the world is but a pseudochurch.

A scientist once said: "Verity is a thing all the world chases after but never discovers." The more man learns of space and life the more he knows that verities are further from defining. In the face of man's incertitude the church must proclaim without hesitation before any power or authority the supremacy and the total applicability of God's wisdom for all of life.

The world has an excess of self-confident people—each pushing ahead for himself—of whom the psalmist wrote:

> When his breath departs he returns to his earth;
> on that very day his plans perish. (Ps. 146:4 RSV)

But God's child, knowing he belongs to God and is sent out by God, has God-confidence instead of self-confidence. Dauntless as John the Baptist he may say: "He must grow greater and greater and I less and less" (John 3:30 Phillips). He carries jewels from a treasure chest of infinitely varied riches. Because he knows that treasure is unlimited he does not hoard. He tells everyone where it is found.

Where is the boundary of universes with their galaxies, suns, and planets? Where is the limit to God's knowing? Each new vision of science and experience reveals new wonders in God's wisdom for every human problem. Each new day, lived toward God, reveals new vistas of his plan.

How great thy wisdom, God, our Father, for every moment of existence! Give us humility of faith to live by it. Give us temerity of love to make it known in every place of influence and authority. Amen.

A DESIGN CARRIED THROUGH

3:11 *In line with the design of the ages which he put into effect through Christ Jesus our master!*

God's way and wisdom are always true to what God is. His meaning is effected and made clear by Jesus Christ. As Christ masters us, we are led in God's way; we apply his wisdom to every sphere of life.

God's way and wisdom are not far-off ideals, but the real in action. Every man knows of his own wisdom that "if to do were as easy as to know what were good to do, chapels had been churches, and poor men's cottages princes' palaces." [7] God knows what to do, for he made the field of doing and the possibility for doing. God knows what to do, and he does it. We see, to our embarrassment, what he is about as we look at the meaning of Jesus Christ. Human schemes deteriorate. Old systems vanish. God's design proceeds toward fulfillment.

Although the design is good, if the materials be at fault, how shall it endure? A design in sands of time is washed away. A design in wood of human artifice may burn up. God's design in Jesus Christ is for never ending ever. Jesus Christ is the pattern of God's design.

And in Jesus Christ we see our human part in God's design. By Jesus Christ we test our contribution to it (I Cor. 3:13). A disillusioned revolutionary discovered "immoral means produce immoral ends." [8] There is no way except by him who is the way. We can know what Paul knew when he wrote: "To those who love God, who are called according to his plan, everything that happens fits into a pattern for good" (Rom. 8:28 Phillips). He plans. He calls us. We respond. He fits us to his pattern. Then, whatever happens in human happenstance or temporal circumstance, his love works through us as it worked through Jesus Christ, square with his total, over-all design.

Dear Father, thy design, effected in our elder brother Jesus Christ, effect in us. We yield ourselves to thee to be used in thy plan for the ages. Amen.

CONFIDENCE IN GOD

3:12 Joined to him (Jesus Christ, our master), we are reassured in him, and thus come to God with confidence, trusting in him.

We come to God with confidence.

A new boy in school had broken the rules and knew he must be corrected. Sent to the principal's office he stood outside the door afraid to knock. His teacher, whom he knew to be his friend, opened the door and introduced the boy to the principal. The boy found that the principal was, like the teacher, his friend. They stood firmly against infractions, not for the sake of the rules, but for the sake of the boys. They were against wrongdoing, but they were for him. Through the following years they inspired and guided him to maturity.

There is no complicated combination to unlock the door between God and us. Christ is the key. In Christ we see what God is like. We see his anger at sham and at shameless insensitivity to others. God's love judges us, and his love draws us. His love purges us, his love compels us, his love brings us to his presence.

God-confidence replaces the pretense of self-confidence. Braggadocio is the counterfeit of security. Insecurity is lack of stance in anything sure. In Christ we are assured with the assurance of experience which is ours when we act by trust in him. Anxiety is the nature of self-oriented existence. Trust is the character of God-oriented daily living. Genuine confidence in God grows with commitment to his meaning seen in Christ.

We rely on him. Everything else eventually fails, crumbles away. God never does. He made us. He made life. He made eternity. We are in his plan. His strength strengthens us. His wisdom guides us.

Trusting in Christ, we come to thee, Father! We are relieved that thou, Creator, art judge of our lives and thou, Eternal One, art commander of our destinies. Amen.

GOD COMES REAL

3:13 *So I ask you not to be discouraged by my troubles for you—by which God becomes real to you.*

For God to become real in human lives is worth any trouble, pain, or sacrifice.

Poet James Russell Lowell wrote:

> By the light of burning martyrs,
> Christ, thy bleeding feet we track,
> Toiling up new Calvaries ever
> With the cross that turns not back.

Therefore, do not be disheartened, the letter writer says, when Christ's followers suffer. Have we complained: "So-and-so was good! How could God let him suffer?" Then we have not understood Christ's God. He let Jesus die on the cross. He let Paul suffer many afflictions. He lets those faithful to him in totalitarian states be subjected to psychological whipping. He lets those loyal to Christ's way in nontotalitarian countries be ostracized for their advocacy of love in social relations. But no, he does not just *let* them suffer. Jesus suffered, others have suffered, we may suffer, by choice—by choosing God's design instead of man's disorder. Creation out of chaos always takes effort, often comes with pain. A great creative act is worth the trouble. The greatest creative act of love by which God becomes real—this is worth even the Cross.

Take heart in this, then, that through the Cross God's love prevails. Through human faithfulness to him, God's reality becomes the splendor of life.

So John Bowring could write:

> In the cross of Christ I glory,
> Towering o'er the wrecks of time.

We are not afraid, our God, when we turn our lives toward thee. We know what men have endured to bring thy gospel to us, and we are ready to endure, for thou art with us. Thou art most real, unchanging, always remaining, always leading. Lead thou us on in thy design. Amen.

GOD, THE FATHER

3:14 This is the reason I fall on my knees before the Father.

In prayer to God we refer ourselves to his orders.

We admit God in our lives, we admit his plan. We accept our part in his plan. Our part of the plan involves others. Others must know of God, of his gracious love, wisdom, power for life. Others must do their part that God's design become effective in all the world.

This is the reason the letter writer writes his prayer. He had surrendered his life to the meaning of God—to Christ. He had brought Christ's message to his fellow men. His prayer is for those who follow after. We are all responsible for those who follow after. If we are Christ's, we wish for them his goodness.

In fulfilling his task Paul suffered much (II Cor. 11:23-29). Affliction never made him bow to those who brought affliction. He bowed only to God in whose service he was afflicted. Affliction never made him pity himself. It only made him the more concerned for those for whom he bore affliction. He fell on his knees in acquiescence to God's lordship in his life. This very acquiescence was at the same time a request in behalf of others. Christlike prayer is surrender of self and sincere regard for others.

Thus prayer is referring ourselves to God's orders. Prayer is longing that God's will of love and power and wisdom be known to all. Prayer is preparation to make God's purposes and arrangements known. Prayer becomes action in community with God for the unity of his creation (3:10).

Father, we stand aware of thee because of those who in the past have shared thee with us. We kneel before thee to receive thy love and thy command to share thy will with all mankind. Amen.

THE FATHER AND HIS FAMILY

3:15 . . . *From whom his whole family—gathered to him and scattered in the world—has its identity.*

In God alone is there sense and meaning for people here and everywhere—now and always.

We are members of God's family. Our value lies not in ourselves but in our family relationship—with God and with each other. We are not dependent on possessions and achievement for status in our neighborhood. We do not need a genealogy, or personal connections, or a "right side of town" in which to have our residence, or offices and honors, or a reputation of respectability to satisfy our need to be someone. Value for us is found in our relationship with God's people as children with them of our Father.

Jesus advised Pilate that his position and power were temporarily permitted to him from God (John 19:11). Every power on earth is permitted and temporary. Every group relationship on earth is permitted and temporary. The fixed power, unchanging, is only God's. The eternal relationship, always enduring, is unity with him as Father.

The deeply personal significance here is the fulfillment of our creaturehood. All creation yearns for the creator. There is, for all, a deep subconscious tug toward him. Instinctively we recognize that we are nothing without him. Like satellites flung into existence, we can but swing in orbit around the flame of his love. Cold and lonely is every life that ignores him. But when our hearts cry out, "Father, God!" we know that we are his. "Knowledge of God is knowledge of living with God." [9] In his fellowship we know who we are and understand our fellow men and engulf them in the goodwill of God. Everything about us changes. He changes not. He *is.* We are his.

In him and his we find identity.

Father, God who made us, make us truly thine. Our one-with-another oneness with thee no time shall change, nor distance separate; for we are one in thine eternal love. Amen.

INNER STRENGTH

3:16 May God give you from his rich realness the capacity for inward strength enabled by his spirit.

Enduring strength comes from God.

God's acts are positive. His gifts are positive, clear, sure. Our reception of his gifts, however, is often tentative.

Our tentativeness may be our desire to have God's gifts alone, for our self-willed plans, for our self-anxieties. God's greatest gift is given to us as members of his family with whom we are related. It comes to us to enable us to share it with those about us with whom we must relate. Our relations with the world God loves can be significant only when his gift to us marks our relationship with him.

When God's rich realness becomes a part of our lives, we become more richly real to others. We understand others, and they see our integrity when we have accepted from God the capacity to be. The daily practice of God's realness in our thoughts and acts develops the capacity he gives us to be real persons.

Our acts among and for others are significant only as they are a part of our becoming what God intends us to become. God's people, strengthened by his spirit, determined by his will, are freed to love with his love.

Father, by thy spirit strengthen us inwardly, that we may be thy people, carrying out thy plans. Amen.

71

ROOTED IN LOVE

3:17 As you rely on him, may Christ live in your hearts. May your lives be rooted and grounded in love.

Trusting Christ, God's meaning, we have stability.

Reliance on Christ is not hiding away in a dreamworld of nice religion. It is action in fellowship with those committed to his living purpose. His purpose attacks to conquer every phase of God's creation.

Reliance on Christ is living by a common trust in God who is among us. Christ is at the heart of our comradeship in his church. He is the permanence for whom we shed our transiency. He is the gatherer for whom we surrender our separateness. He is the love that binds us from disunity, that his spirit in us may bind the world from its divisiveness. His love is like the ocean tide that fills the little pools beside the beach, and they become part of the sea. The sea resides in the heart of each pool; so may his love in us.

Hereby we know the church, if love resides in it. It is the love that goes beyond itself to all the world.

Cut flowers do not grow. Nor do rootless people grow in vases of sentimental religion. Rooted flowers grow. Rooted trees shall not be moved by every breeze that blows. But for him who knows not why he lives much of existence wastes away. He tosses with the winds. He goes after mirages. Excitements may be knocking him about. He has no roots. He cannot grow.

Windblown in search of truth, we do not grow. Trusting God whose way we see in Christ, however, firmly rooted in his love, we grow. Sure of God's love, living by his strength, grounded to his eternal goodwill, we are established by his total meaning.

Father, we put our trust completely in thee. May Christ reside among us and reach the whole world through us. May we be rooted in thy love, firmly fixed in it. Amen.

TO GRASP AT LOVE

3:18 . . . So that you might be strong enough to grasp for yourself—in company with all God's consecrated people—what the breadth, the length, the height, the depth of Christ's love may be!

To be strong enough to grasp the heart of meaning is to reach for him who reaches us!

Life's full dimensions are found in God's Christlike love. Here is room for all. Yet here is no room for hate and fear, or for deceit that cheats a fellow man, these defenses of the self-centered.

The self-centered are off-center, far off from the heart of God. The art of loving is an artifice when it is servant to crippled self-concern. They love to be loved. They win friends to influence them.

God's love, fully expressed in Christ, is the creative core of life. The letter writer prays that his readers have strength to grasp it. This takes effort. Human love is frail. Like black coffee or pep pills there are stimuli to goodwill which counterfeit strength. Religious revivals or political rallies may rouse emotions of goodwill which ebb before tides of distrust or human weariness.

The strength to grasp the love of Christ is our strength doubled. An unexpected stranger came from God to Jacob and wrestled with him. Jacob would not let him go until the man had "blessed him" (Gen. 32:22-30). Love comes to us from God, an unexpected stranger to our way of life. God's love cannot be ours until we exert our determined best that it bless, or saturate, our lives. His love entices us to reach, encourages us to dare, enables us to think and to believe.

When we rise to the love that reaches us, our lives are stretched, extended, statured, rooted. That love is broader than the universe, longer than time, higher than hope. The depth of human experience cannot contain the whole of it.

God, in the midst of life thy universal love has found us. By its strength enlarge our hearts, extend our minds. Together with thy people let us penetrate with love to every area, every corner of human existence. Amen.

TO MATURE IN LOVE

3:19 . . . So that you might know the love of Christ, which is more than all knowledge; so that you might be mature in the maturity which is of God!

God's love matures us.

In place of substitutes for ignorance, instead of escape religion for misfits, God's love fills up the empty places of our understanding, the lonely places in our relationships. It stirs the mind to large appreciations for this life. It sends the heart outreaching in gratitude for fellow men.

This is the love men saw expressed in Jesus' life. It is the love that extended to the Cross. It is the love of God become one with man to lift man to eternal and all-including fellowship.

This love is more than knowledge. "A man certain of God's love can afford to be uncertain of much else." [10] It goes beyond knowledge in giving depth, stability, wholeness, and stature to our lives.

This love is better than knowledge. It provides foundation for intelligent faith uncramped by narrow dogmas. It forms a broad consistency in behavior and in attitudes toward all. It furnishes the mortar for enduring human fellowship.

It is the very wholeness of God which completes the incompleteness of our lives. It is the rhythm by which our lives are synchronized with those who are dominated by his purpose. His purpose itself is love.

We join our prayers, God, to this letter's prayer for us that all thy people may know thy love in Christ, and that their lives and ours may be complete in love, mature in the maturity that comes from thee. Amen.

POWER OF THE REAL

3:20 Now to him who by the exertion of his power among us can do far more than we would ask or conceive.

We had not dreamed life could be like this.

Those first shot into space saw beauty no human eyes had seen before. It awed them. None, bound to their earthly safety, would see this.

When we allow God's thrust of love to send us from ourselves into the spacious life of faith, no longer earthbound, we find a glory in life unguessed before. Our animal wants did not desire it. Our intellectual ideals did not conceive of it.

Here is space uncircumscribed! This is too vast for tiny minds that rest in the security of narrow creeds. Here is power unlimited. This is too dangerous for timid minds that trust in systems to protect their personal interests and group pride. Here is treasure unmeasurable. This is too much for tidy minds that consider Providence a bank account for their prosperity and health.

The potentialities of faith are conditioned by our willingness to accept faith. The force and meaning of love are only for the brave enough to carry out its implications. The possibilities of God are only for the bold enough to apply them to the social, moral order.

Christ is God's creative energy among us. His energy is exerted through his church when the church permits his spirit to attack the depravity of our respectable faults, to humble our petty virtues and anemic goodness, to tear from us our well-adjusted selfhood and break the shell of our complacent chrysalis.

The wonder of his love walks with us through troubles, griefs, and conflicts—through time, through death, and through eternity.

Power of God, we would dare step out of our hiding place unarmed, undefended, from thy love. Give us the bravery to live beyond our systemized good works. Work thou, Great Power, dynamically through us. Amen.

THE SPLENDOR OF THE REAL

3:21 . . . To him may his splendor (seen in the church and in Christ Jesus) direct attention through all the generations and through all time. May it truly be so!

He is the focus of all that is real.

He is the never-ending wonder by which, for which, we live.

In a tumult of chatter and laughter English school girls on tour walked through a college hallway in Oxford. They pushed open the door of its great library and fell abruptly quiet, in awe at its grandeur. One girl exclaimed for all: "Smashing!" Himalayan hikers rounded a bend at twelve thousand feet and saw the sudden sunlit splendor of pillared Mt. Kedarnath. They were stunned to silent admiration.

Here is the greatest wonder open to man's amazement: the beauty, the power, the full adequacy of God. Such splendor for all life and time! Men saw this wonder in Christ. Christ pointed men to God, directed their attention to him, reflected his realness. The church exists for this.

The church exists to reflect the reality of God and to wake men from their dreams and nightmares to the realism of God. The church that *is* the church directs its thoughts to God, lives expectantly for him. Such a church puts the world in mind of him who is genuine and real. The sham and show of society apart from God is hard to live in, impossible to live by. The televiewer, the consumer citizen, might well echo the sick philosopher who said, "Ah, how I am weary of all the inadequate that is insisted on as actual!" [11]

The power and adequacy, the presence and splendor of God needs no insistence. For he is the focus of all that is real for those who live by him. And their lives together in his church cannot but direct attention to him through every generation and through all time.

O God, may it truly be this way: that we will reflect the love of Christ. May the world's attention be directed beyond itself and beyond thy church to thee and so be restored to thee and to thy purpose. Amen.

THE CONDUCT OF THE CALLED

4:1 *As a prisoner bound to the Master, I call on you to conduct yourselves in a manner that befits the summons you have received.*

Our lives are to reflect the unity to which God calls us.

This letter is concerned with the nature and the preservation of the unity God intends. In our world uniformity is being forced by fear. Unity, however—the unity of trust in and concern for one another—is brought about by love. Love is from the Father, and it has demonstrated itself in Jesus Christ.

We, too, are called on to demonstrate the unity of love. The word "call" which the letter writer uses had three meanings: an invitation, a command, a summons. God invites us to accept his fellowship. He commands us to obey his purpose. He summons us to attend the consummation he designed.

Our acceptance of his invitation, our obedience to his command, our attendance on his summons are indicated in our behavior. Jesus told the story of a wedding guest ejected from the wedding because he had not dressed for the occasion. His carelessness was an insult to his host. A careless, nominal attitude to God is an insult to the meaning of our creation. "Let your light shine in the sight of men," said Jesus—the light God gives you. "Be like your Father, mature," said Jesus. Reflect him who has honored you by inviting you to be his people. In older times no Spartan would flinch at suffering, for he was a Spartan. No Roman would run from the enemy, for he was a Roman. No knight would forsake those dependent on him, for he was a knight. No Samurai would desert his lord, for he was a Samurai. And today no follower of Christ dare fail his calling, for he is Christ's. He acts in a manner suitable to his calling.

We who live in the spirit of Christ, like Christ, are prisoners of God's love.

God, our Father, because we are thine, make us, like Christ, prisoners of thy love. Arrest our scattered lives and confine us within the bounds of thine unbounded love. Amen.

LIVE IN LOVE

4:2 *Live among yourselves in love for one another with complete humility and genuine courtesy.*

The test of God's love among us is the way we live with one another.

His love among us acts through the will, not through emotion. It is reasonable. It is objective. In his love we accept others, not for ourselves but for themselves. His love among us is shown in complete humility and in genuine courtesy. It is forgiveness that forbears.

Humility is humble-mindedness. A psychoanalyst writes, "To be objective, to use one's reason, is possible only if one has achieved an attitude of humility." [1] Only in humility are the blinds taken off the eyes so that we can see and understand each other.

Humility is freedom from false facades.

> And we confess our blame,
> That all too high we hold
> That noise which man calls fame
> That dross which man calls gold. [2]

Genuine courtesy is freedom from passion. He who has nothing but himself displays himself. He who has God's possession of himself needs no display. He depends on no affection. At its core his life, dispassionate, is solid, steadfast, calmly glad—rooted in God's love.

There are many imitation gems in the world. They may be flashy. Real gems glow. Their sparkle reflects light deep within the stone. True considerateness is clearer than superficial politeness. The imitation man is frothful, the real man is fruitful (Gal. 5:22).

The fellowship of God's church—the promise of his future —are those who live with each other in love, in complete humility, in genuine courtesy.

We walk into the house of thy love, our Father. Disrobe us of all pretense. We want to live in thy presence, among the fellow men thou givest us, in complete humility and genuine courtesy. Amen.

FORGIVENESS THAT FORBEARS

4:2 . . . *Patiently bearing with one another.*

The test of God's love among us is the way we live with one another.

Patience that endures holds on. Patience bears up "when others try to dominate you, prey on you, take advantage of you, strike you in the face" (II Cor. 11:20). "He is not truly patient who will only suffer so much as he thinks good, and from whom he pleases."

Patience holds on in difficulties. Refugees who marched to a gruelling pace through jungled mountains in Burma and Assam during wartime and held on reached safety. Followers of Christ, following his track, hold one another up, hold out for God's purpose.

Patience holds on when ridiculed, ostracized, or persecuted for faith (I Cor. 4:12). A missionary nurse bore up under the torture and brainwashing of a bandit group in North Korea. "Many soldiers," she later reported, "died in concentration camps for no other reason than that, under the constant bombardment of propaganda, they had nothing to hold on to."

Forgiveness that forbears holds on. A mother can bear patiently the screams of a child in pain or distress because she loves that child. Her patience is concern. Strangers would be irritated. To the extent we love, to that extent we bear with others patiently. Short of love, we are short of patience. Nerves, especially tired nerves, are easily frayed. Irritated persons quickly run out of patience. Love does not suppress irritation. It outruns it.

It is among these, the patient to endure, the forgiving to forbear, that God lives. For he says,

> I dwell in the high and holy place,
>   and also with him who is of a contrite and humble spirit,
> to revive the spirit of the humble
>   and to revive the heart of the contrite. (Isa. 57:15 RSV)

Live among us, Father. As thou dost bear with us in love, so let us bear with one another in thy love. We would hold one another up in thee, and find in thee each other. Amen.

UNITY OF SPIRIT

4:3 I call on you to do your part to maintain the unity of the spirit that brings you together in harmony.

We are each a partner in unity. Our oneness is the unity of our manyness.

Enduring unity within us, among us, about us, comes when we are bound by a common conviction in dedication to God's spirit. His spirit unites. His spirit controls. Like thread that holds a garment together—and the garment warms! Like thought that holds the phrases of a sentence together—and the sentence communicates! Like the hypothalamus in the brain that regulates and controls many functions of the body in a unified constancy, that regulates and controls the behavior of the individual in respect to his environment! So the spirit binds our manyness in love's oneness—and relates our oneness to the world! Love binds us against unlove, whose breed of prejudice and selfishness distorts, divides.

Such unity is willed for in endeavor, not wished for in our dreams. Such peace is purchased in mutual self-surrender, not purloined through self-imposition. God's spirit gives no unity but what we are ready to keep. His power provides no peace but what we are eager to maintain. He binds nothing but what we yield to him.

So the letter writer says: "Keep unity in the spirit." So Jesus said: "Keep on forgiving." Unity is sealed by deeds. It is sewn together by attitudes, woven through daily expressions. It is fellowship not only with those like us but with those unlike us. It is goodwill for a friend, but also for a stranger, for the lovely but also for the unlovely, for the ally but also for the enemy.

Spirit of God, attach us to thyself! Attach us to one another in thee. Spirit of God, fill us with thy love. Flow over us and mingle us in the flood of thy goodwill. Amen.

UNITED IN HOPE

4:4 You are called together into one body and in one spirit by the very fact that God's call unites you in one hope.

God's call gives us unity.

We, the church, are the community of those who know God has called them. This is not a fellowship resulting from man's desire for togetherness. It is brought into being by God's will for his final community. The only basis for our oneness is God's choice of us, his will for us, his purpose through us. Our unity is maintained when we are directed by his spirit.

God's spirit, not man's organization, gives the church life. A living body is the completion of its parts. A living body is what Paul called the many in one body in Christ (Rom. 12:5). The living body of God's church is whole, alive, and sound. It is his living event in time—sure and certain.

We, his people, when we *are* his, are one body, animated by one spirit, under one influence. Our attitudes toward all are determined by his attitude toward us and our attitude toward him: an attitude of love. Love is indivisible.

Words are gathered sensefully into a sentence, and sentences into chapters, and chapters into a book that tells a complete story. We are the words of God's book: his story. His story is an announcement of a program that will be consummated because it is already being consummated. And we are a part of its consummation. This is our hope: we expect God's purpose will be fulfilled. We are like people gathered for the opening of a great event. We live in the dawn, looking for the first streaks of God's new day. Our hope illuminates the suppositions by which we live.

In answering thy call, O God, we place all our hopes in thee. Thy presence draws us together, unites us in thy spirit. Amen.

4:5 *We have one Master, one allegiance, one commitment.*

We, the church, all have one Master and to him we all are bound in one loyalty and by one dedication.

We have one Master. He is the one supreme link to whom we all are joined. He possesses us. He has the ultimate authority over each of us. He has the right to dispose of our lives together for his purpose. He is our Lord.

We have one allegiance. We are, as his church, all attached to him. We heed *him,* obey *him,* in all we do. Our loyalty to him stirs us to the thoughts we think, to the deeds we do. Our lives comply with his will. We trust in him, rely on him. We live with confidence in him. This loyalty, this faith, is more than an attitude of belief. It is "an act of the whole person, of mind, will, and heart. Faith is *sensitivity, understanding, engagement,* and *attachment.*" [3]

We have one commitment. Commitment means to be immersed in the spirit of Christ. Baptism was, to early followers of Christ, the symbol of our unity in him. It was the door through which all entered the one household of faith, of commitment to our one Lord. It symbolized the sharing by each follower in the spirit of Christ. In other words, commitment meant submerging the self in the purpose of God in Christ to draw the world to him. We are renewed for a new usage—his. Our passionate selves are plunged like red-hot steel in the coolness of his objective compassion. He tempers us. He hardens flabby sentiment to courageous commitment.

Thus we are, in him who is one, made one, one people with one Lord.

We commit our lives to thee, our Master. Remake us to thy will. Bring us to the unity that always comes to thy people when thy people come to thee. Amen.

ONE GOD AND FATHER

4:6 *We have the one God, the Father of all of us, who is ruler over all of us and who creates through all of us and is present among all of us.*

We, the church, are God's family, God's palace, God's workshop, God's temple.

God is one. The test of our relatedness to God is, then, our unity, for God is not divided among us.

God is the Father of all of us even though all have not yet become aware of this fact. The church—his church—recognizes this relationship and lives by it. Thereby the relationship becomes dynamic.

God is ruler over all of us. Hence, nothing is to supersede him in our lives. Awareness of his authority in our lives saves us from childish submission to the anonymous authority of public opinion and of commercially instilled public tastes or politically instigated public passion.

God is creator through us. Our own opinions, tastes, and compassion are influenced by the action of his spirit on our minds and relationships. So are our decisions and our acts. If the stone had feelings, the sculptor's hammer and chisel would hurt the stone. If the stone had flaws, the sculptor's plans would now and then be checked by them. So are we hurt sometimes and sometimes hinder God's creating process. Yet if we remain patiently in God's hands, his action among us creates—and the beauty of his design becomes apparent.

God is present among us. We, his church, become the forum for his spirit, reasoning with us and with the world. We, his church, become the court of his judgment on us and on the world. We cannot escape him if we are his church. Like seeping dampness in wet weather God permeates his living church.

> "O Lord and Master of us all:
>   Whate'er our name or sign,
> We own thy sway, we hear thy call,
>   We test our lives by thine! Amen." [4]

EACH HAS A PART

4:7 To each one of us has been given a share of God's gracious goodwill as his part of the gift of Christ.

Each of us has his distinct part in God's action of goodwill.

God's plan for unity is made up of our diversity. We are reminded here that, in the unity of the growing, living body of Christ's church, we each have different talents to contribute and functions to perform. The applications of our talents and our functions have their vital force from Christ, who is our head. We are like the network of canals that reaches out across the plains from a great river. Our water is from one great river of life, but each has a special place and time for bringing that water to the parched ground.

God's gift to all of us comes through our awareness of Jesus' gracious love, his generous design for man. We each, as God has made it possible, can demonstrate in particular ways this his gracious will.

In this way our several gifts contribute to his plan. Many flowers may bloom from a single plant. And from each flower may come the seed of another plant. We grow from him in many ways to serve his cause and fructify his purpose.

But, whatever our talent and our function, if they are from God, they reflect his gift of Christ. It is, like him, gracious, generous, goodwilled.

Yet we must remember that all of us as partners in his plan assist and still depend on one another as we share his goodwill. Our tasks are supplemental to each other's.

Father, we thank thee for thy gracious goodwill to all of us. We thank thee for thy particular gifts to each of us. May we each do our appointed tasks in the spirit of Christ. Amen.

THE GIFT OF A GREAT TASK

4:8 *For we are told: "He has gone up to the height.*
He has caught his captives.
He has given gifts to men."

Such things used to happen long ago: conquering kings returned to their capitals with an entourage of captives, receiving tribute gifts from the conquered. Such things happen
yet: peoples are "liberated" from old empires and enslaved to
new powers with new ideologies.

The ancient Jewish people hoped such things would happen again. The conquering king would be their lord, Messiah, and his coming would be up to the heights of Mt. Zion.
The uniting of his people under him would follow (Ps. 68:
18-27). One way or another, many modern men hope, such
things will happen again. They are ready to follow anyone
who promises salvation from suffering and humiliation. Such
things are happening. They are movements forced by fear.
They last awhile. They fail.

Here is a movement forced by love. It fills all human need.
It lasts, will last, always. Our letter writer saw it in Jesus'
mission. Jesus quoted Isaiah for his mission: "I have come,"
he said, "to set the captives free."

Here is a greater, more enduring conquest pictured. Christ
captures us who were captive to evil and makes us his. We
were subject to ourselves, to our surroundings, to our sins.
We were slaves to our times and our times' weakness. By the
power of his person, by love, Christ sets us free. In doing
so he captivates us. The very love that saved us from ourselves
now sends us out to others under his command.

He demands no tribute, for he needs none. It is *he* who
gives the gifts. The gifts he gives are opportunities to do our
tasks in his great task. We are now not only under the authority of God, but we can act with his authority.

God, capture us. Take us from fear to faith, from despair to
hope, from entanglement in ourselves to service to thyself.
Give us the disciplined spirit of the courageous, compassionate,
conquering Christ. Amen.

HE COMES TO US TO GO WITH HIM

4:9 But what does it mean: "He went up," if not that he had already gone down into the heart of our world?

He comes to us in all our meanness that we may find his meaningfulness.

The ancient rule of kings was this: Who comes back victorious, first goes out valorous. Ancient religious men used to say: a prince of life will someday come down to free men from evil, then reign supreme in all the universe (Col. 2:15).

The early churchmen said: Jesus actually lived the life of God among us. He overcame demonic power in our lives. He revealed to us what is supreme in all the universe. In him we see God come to man to take man to himself.

We sense this, too. He lives and moves among us. He is no high God far removed, eternally distant in his authority, rapt in bliss. He is our God in that he is concerned about our human need, our suffering, our aspiration. God is above us because he is among us. He transcends because he descends—to the scum of our individual sin and to the slum of our social sin —to take us to the house of his purity, to the city of God. There are no "lower depths" of existence where he is not present, no higher heights of intellect where he is not found (Ps. 139:7-12). He overtops everything for us because he undergirds everything for us. He dominates us because he penetrates us. He breaks in on our crowded isolation, intrudes on our mass privacy, invades our social selfishness. He conquers us and captures us.

He leads us from where we were to where he is.

Today, O God, we acknowledge thy victory over every phase and facet of existence. Surround us, secure us, save us from our wretchedness; save us for the greatness of thy purpose. Amen.

FULL OF MEANING

4:10 *The very one who went down, went up to fill the universe with his presence.*

His meaning fills existence, all of it for us.

He does not let us down. He fulfills our basic need to be. He fills his church. He fills our world, and all experience comes together in significance when he is master of our lives.

He comes to us to bring us to himself.

> Light looked down and beheld darkness.
> "Thither will I go," said Light.
> Peace looked down and beheld war.
> "Thither will I go," said Peace.
> Love looked down and beheld hatred.
> "Thither will I go," said Love.
> So came Light, and shone.
> So came Peace, and gave rest.
> So came Love, and brought life.
> And the Word was made flesh, and dwelt among us.[5]

"He dwelt among us" and thereby let us become sons and daughters of God. "He dwelt among us" and thereby let us become brothers and sisters to each other. He made the problem of getting along with people a practice in creative living. We are all in the same boat, but he mans the boat.

He dwells among us and thereby transfigures every perception.

> And deep below the deeps of conscious being,
> Thy splendor shineth; there, O God, Thou art.[6]

For he empties us of ourselves and fills us with himself. Self blinded us; he opens our eyes.

We now can use the Hebrew poet's words: "My cup overflows!" God fills the cup of life to overflowing. He fills our minds and consciousness with his presence.

Father, we gladly witness the wonder of thy presence. We gratefully perceive the fullness of thy meaning for all of life. Fill our world of experience with reminders of thyself. Amen.

PARTICULAR RESPONSIBILITIES

4:11 *He himself gave the appointments: some to be his official messengers.*

To each of us in his church he has given a particular task.

For the church is like a bridge from God to man. The bridge is made of many parts: of towers, cables, wires, and steel suspension ropes, bolts, rivets, and concrete. The church is made of many people. They are its many parts.

His appointments are his gifts to us. God's gifts are not presents to satisfy us for our pleasure. God's gifts are talents to qualify us for his purpose. *He* makes the appointments. *We* accept. The art, in faith, is to learn from God what he has given us to do. And then to do it.

The letter writer classified some of the tasks in the church in his day. Some churchmen in his day had the stamp of official message bearers. The disciples who had been with Jesus were looked upon as official authorities in the church. Their closeness to Jesus—or their life in Christ—seemed to give them insights many did not have. People in the church looked to them for counsel.

Among us are some who live so conscious of God's presence and his wisdom that their lives can counsel others and make them aware of Jesus' ministry, mission, and meaning. They have a sense of mission to make God's purpose clear in some special problem, in some special place within his church.

Many of us at one time or another may be commissioned by God's spirit to bring his message to bear on some area of life. It may be to some neighbor family or some group in town. It may be to some need far away. It may be to strengthen with love the faith within the church. It may be to work for Christ-like change in social life and in human relations. When commissioned we must act. But we must never forget: the ambassador never acts but by and according to the instructions of the one who sends him. His authority is delegated and must be used responsibly.

We thank thee, Father, for thy gifts. We thank thee for responsibilities thou givest us within thy church. We thank thee for those among us who bring us nearer to thee. Amen.

BY WORD OF MOUTH

4:11 . . . *Some to be spokesmen for him, others to pro-claim his good news.*

God has spokesmen for him in the church.

Some people are gifted with the ability to help others understand God's will and its application to their lives. Today we may call them "preachers." Any member of Christ's church may come to an experience that inspires him with new understanding of God's will in his life and perhaps in the congregation's life. In such a case he shares his understanding with others. God's spokesman must never allow his ego to be mixed up with what he says for God. He is willing that all he says be tested by God's love.

God's spokesman speaks for him not only in the congregation of the church. He may be moved to deliver God's message to the world outside the church. He speaks to the church commending it to obedience in God's will. He speaks to the world condemning it for disobedience to God's judgment. He explains to the world the nature of God's plan and the consequence of human disobedience to that plan. But unless the church is a body obedient to its head—to Christ—the spokesman speaks in vain.

God has tellers of good news in the church. "Tellers of good news" (evangelists) announced the message of Christ to those who had not heard it. This designation still has importance when the church fulfills its function to carry Christ's message to the world. Anyone is an evangelist who cannot keep to himself his joy over the good news that he has heard. This good news, of course, is that God, in Jesus Christ, reconciles our lives to him and re-creates us to a new humanity. This good news can be expressed through multivarious forms of human thought and living.

> *"Lord, speak to me, that I may speak*
> *In living echoes of thy tone;*
> *As thou hast sought, so let me seek*
> *Thine erring children lost and lone." Amen.*[7]

TO GUARD AND GUIDE THE CHURCH

4:11 . . . *And others to watch over and teach us.*

God has made others guardians and instructors in the faith.

The shepherd used to live with his sheep and guard them from all danger. New converts from the pagan world needed protection from ungodly customs. They needed guidance in their faith. Guardians are needed now. Television and press, advertisements, customs, and pastimes all could divert us from the practice of our faith when that faith is weak. We need to heed the concern of Christ's followers for our lives. We need to take with patience their rebukes and to weigh their advice. We need, as well, to avoid the cowardice of silence when we see waywardness among the people of God. We must speak truthfully in a loving spirit, but we must speak. We are our brothers' keepers because we are our brothers' brothers.

We need teachers to instruct us. Early teachers in the church explained men's experiences of God as recorded in Judaic scriptures. They told the story of Jesus' teaching and compassion. They interpreted in these the significance of God's love for the world (John 3:16; Rom. 5:8; II Cor. 5:18-19). We need to be taught again and again these bases of our faith. We need to be led to rethink deeply the motivations of our lives.

We need, also, to learn that we may teach others. We teach others not to make them imitators of our customs, repeaters of our doctrines, or parrots of our formulas. The teacher in the church tells his pupils about the work of God and confronts them with the life of Christ. The teacher in the church leaves to God's spirit the forming of Christ in his pupils' minds and hearts.

> "O teach me, Lord, that I may teach
> The precious things thou dost impart;
> And wing my words, that they may reach
> The hidden depths of many a heart." Amen.[8]

SERVICE IN HIS CHURCH

4:12 These appointments were given so as to fit God's people for the work of service—for their conduct of his church: "the body of Christ."

We are gifted, each in some way, not to profit ourselves but to enrich each other. Our tasks within God's church fit together in mutual service so that we can be a whole church with a wholesome message for the world.

For the church is—by definition in the letters collected in the New Testament—people who are consecrated to God, whose lives are used for his purpose. We are his tools, set to toil for him in a variety of ways. We do not postpone service until tomorrow, nor merely look for popular causes to join. The service he assigns us is to be good neighbors now, always, wherever we may be. God gives us each what some neighbor needs. God also gives us neighbors who serve our needs.

Service, then, is no condescending spare-time act of benevolence. Service is obedience to him who rules us. He who rules his church is love. Love rules us. We are love's menials. We wait on love; we follow in his attendance. At his bidding we wash the roadside dust from tired feet—all tired feet are his. At love's bidding we share our bread with hungry men, our homes with homeless children. Their hunger is his. Their homelessness is his.

We follow him who cares for the least of us. We cannot be aloof. We must, as his church, live in the world as he lived among us, for love is practical. Love flies not in clouds but walks in crowds.

His love shows each of us our part. Only by our tasks' variety do we operate his church. For every part of his living body is active to keep alive each other part.

"Take my life, and let it be consecrated, Lord, to thee.
Take my moments and my days; let them flow in ceaseless praise.
Take my hands, and let them move at the impulse of thy love.
Take my feet, and let them be swift and beautiful for thee."
Amen.[9]

MATURITY IN THE CHURCH

4:13 So shall we all at last arrive at the unity inherent in our faith in, and in our knowledge of, the son of God. So shall we all at last reach a maturity measured by the completeness of Christ.

The goal is maturity of the church, and the mark of maturity is unity, and the standard of maturity is Christ.

God provides a way, a road for the church to travel by, that it may reach the destination he has prepared. Only when the church travels that road toward that goal can it be used by God to effect his will in the world. For this reason he has given each of us some gift of service in the church.

"Faith" is receiving the gift he gives. "Knowledge" is thinking in God's direction, looking through the fog that lies around us toward the way his pathway leads.

Faith and knowledge are acting the will of God. Jesus said of faith: "Ask . . . seek . . . knock." We ask for his wisdom, we seek his will, we knock on the door that opens to his way.

Faith is confidence in, and knowledge is attention to, the meaning that God has shown to us through him who demonstrated in his life, in his self-giving, the pattern of God among men. That pattern unifies us. As he is one, so we, moving toward him, are in one company. There are not many roads. There is one road to him. If we travel that road, we travel together. As people's faces reflect the sunset when they look toward it, our lives reflect the consummation we expect.

Like the pieces of a jigsaw puzzle, we make no sense apart from the other pieces. Put together, each in his place, we make a picture—Christ. Christ is our completeness. The church is complete, in other words, only as it portrays Christ—God's love. In a world of many selfish groups—insecure, confused, unstable—the church, if Christ's, stands secure, complete, mature.

We come to thee, O God, as children. In faith's schoolhouse train us toward love's maturity. Lead us to the completeness of Christ. Amen.

MATURITY IN FAITH

4:14 Then we will no longer be babies, agitated, unsteadied, by every pressure of propaganda which tricky and crafty men use to confuse the people.

Marks of immaturity are disunity and confusion, vagaries in knowledge, vacillation in faith.

A baby is easily agitated. He responds emotionally. He does not reason. He reacts to every pressure. He does not yet have a steady, integrating purpose. We too have been like babies in spirit with no sure direction, no balance, no steady hope beyond the moment's circumstance. We've been like autumn leaves blown here and there by every eddying breeze. We've been like seas disturbed by every wind that blows. Conflicting ideals clash in the battles of our minds. Conflicting desires crash against one another in our hearts. We fluctuate between opinions forced on our attention, between clamoring claims upon our time.

Unsettled natures are easily misled. Many of us who are professionally skilled, or apt in the world of trade, are yet illiterate in our faith, cradled in our fears and rocked by prejudice. We've known no more than babies do the good God planned for us.

In our blind alleys lust's panderers would seduce us. In our Vanity Fairs greed's peddlers would solicit us. We are pressed to do whatever is done by the absolute contemporary. Apostles of discord frighten us with suspicions. Mass movements rob the people of their freedom in the name of freedom. They inflame to influence. They cajole to control. They spin ideological dreams to catch the sleepyheaded.

They dread, these demagogues, the strength of unity in Christ. They fear the force of love.

Our Father, hear us. Help us hear thee. In the babel of confusion we listen. Through the wind, earthquake, and fire we listen for thy still, small voice. Amen.

MUTUALITY OF LOVE

4:15 *Maintaining truth with love we shall in everything grow toward him who is the head—Christ himself.*

Joined to Christ, we continue steady.

This is the church he intended. It moves but not in circles, not in scores of directions, not as floating, fluctuating flotsam on the sea of existential circumstance.

His church is movement forward toward fulfillment of God's design. God's design is pure. It is, in other words, true, unmuddied with human guile or greed, or egoistic subterfuge in strife. Clean, clear, transparent, God's purity affects our movement toward him. So we move forward in truth, sincerity.

God's design is love. It is, in other words, objective, undependent, self-giving reverence for every creature. So God's love affects our movement toward him. We move forward with his love for one another.

God's design is the ultimate, the goal. It is, in other words, complete and meaningful. It nourishes our growth as the sun nourishes the plants. So God's ultimacy affects our immediacy. We grow toward him in everything. Our speech, our acts, our habits, work, and leisure, pleasure, and suffering dominated by his truth in love: we'll grow toward him.

God's design is worked through Christ who heads the church. So Christ affects our movement. We move toward him, and that is why, with him, we move together.

The church, steady in holding to truth with love, moves, grows toward him, toward Christ.

Christ be our head! Christ be the focus of our faith! Christ draw us on together, on to full peoplehood of love! O God, we come to thee who has come to us. Amen.

THE WHOLENESS OF LOVE

4:16 *It is from the head [Christ] that the whole body [the church] is joined together, knit together, by the joints and ligaments with which it is provided. The body grows as each individual part functions according to its capacity, and builds itself up in love.*

Christ unites us. Christ controls.

The body is the wholeness of its parts. Directed by its head, powered by its heart, it lives as each part contributes to the life of the whole. The head of the church is Christ; his love, God's love, its heart.

God provides us our relations. We do not choose and have no right to choose whom we will accept and whom reject. God provides us people with whom to work, with whom to live, whom to help and be helped by.

Different as we are, with different backgrounds defining our views, we are bound together in Christ. Christ directs us to work with each other. When a muscle and its tendons tend to overfunction independently, they thereby go into a spasm. Then the physician calls for reciprocal and cooperative exercise so that the tendons and muscle integrate with other tendons and muscles. Thus they work back to smooth functioning. So must the members of Christ's body.

God provides our functions. He makes it possible for each person, each generation, in each situation and in each area of the world, to play some special part co-active with each other. The church, Christ's body, fails to fulfill its function to the extent we fail to fulfill our particular functions. We fail to grow save as we grow along with fellow members "in Christ."

The body is the wholeness of its parts. Each part is limited, but is part of the unlimited whole. The church is like a building in construction. Each of us builds and is built into the whole. God's love is the mortar.

Lord God, lead us by thy love. Let thy love thread through us. Let thy love bind us. Let thy love blend our pieces in thy total pattern. Amen.

A CHANGE OF CONDUCT

4:17 Now, this Christ is our master, I tell you, and, as from him, I charge you: conduct your lives no longer as do people of the world. They live off-center, their minds fixed on futile things.

Step out, step up with God away from wasted living.

Christ makes a difference. He cuts us off from the tortuous past. He is a new direction. Christ is the way away from blind alleys. He is the highway.

The letter writer reminds us, in the next few passages of his letter, what conversion in human society means. It means to turn our backs on Christless patterns of our past. It means as well to turn toward all that can make of us real persons who, together, can be a new real personhood.

The world about us no longer is our fashion plate. We no longer pattern our lives by its manners and customs, nor make its opinions ours. Christ, for us, has become more than a Sunday fancy.

Without God existence is caged living. Without God existence walks up and down in narrow limits. Without God thinking is cramped; it concentrates on futile things. Some people are so busy making a living, it has been said, they have no time to live. Some are so busy, Jesus said, looking for self-fulfillment they lose their very selves. And some are so centered on themselves that they never see the glory of life before them. Trussed by anxieties they are never free for joy.

Away from God existence is off-center. Minds centered on sex, on sensual satisfaction, on possession of things, on status, or on self-pity, have little faculty for intellectual perception. The power to arrive at moral judgment is weak.

Christ opens up caged doors for us and encourages exploration of the mind and aspiration of the human spirit. Christ centers our existence.

Help us, Father, to leap beyond the confused conduct of our past, to walk the way Christ led. Fix our minds on thee. Center our lives. Amen.

A SHADY EXISTENCE

*4:18 Their minds and hearts are disposed to shady things.
They are strangers to the life of God. They are ignorant among
themselves through their hearts' insensitivity.*

Away from God existence is shadowed, unreal, ignorant.

Nevertheless, God made possible a rich, good life capable
of conscious fellowship with him. Yet many exist insensitive
to him, ignorant of what they are, disposed to thoughts and
actions inimical to themselves and opposite to the nature of
the life of God. Potential relationships with God are broken
by these rebellious demagogues, the ego and the appetites.
Rebellion against God is refusal to accept the love wherewith
God would draw us to himself. Rebellion is our indifference
to our creator's claim on us.

We are like physical organs made for vital functions but
turned to stony concretions by drops of calcareous or other
mineral deposits. As a matter of fact, the heart separate from
God is really broken from itself. Pastimes or panaceas may be
applied to cement our fragmented affections, but they may
simply encrust or even petrify our sensibility to the truly
beautiful and joyous things of life. At best, our personalities
may be only patched-up fences that hide the rubbish of
mingled pain and prurience, loneliness and lust.

> For the soul is dead that slumbers
> And things are not what they seem.[10]

Things are not what they seem to those whose lives are
dulled by sedative substitutes for God. They are disposed in
mind and affection toward things that are not clean. Their
understanding of others and their comprehension of the
nature of life dims. For sin (a word for alienation from God)
causes loss of spiritual perceptiveness. A life away from God is
dark. In darkness there is so much stumbling, so much fear, so
much ignorance of what is.

*O God, whose presence is inextinguishable light and joy, en-
lighten us to preceive thee more clearly. We want, Father, all
those who live away from thee to be at home with thee. Amen.*

SEPARATION FROM LIFE

4:19 They have become callous. They have abandoned themselves to sensual living, to impure habits, and to every kind of disregard for the rights of others.

Disregard for God in life is disregard for other selves and disregard for one's own true self.

The letter writer describes those who are too wrapped up in themselves to heed God or to know the place he has for them within his plan. The writer returns to this subject after having told his readers of their place in God's design; he returns to it because he knows the lurking influences of men who leave God out of their lives. Their actions, policies, and habits may still infect the church and make religion, then, a front to secularity.

Callousness results. They cease to sense God's will. They cease to feel their neighbor's needs. They grow insensible to the glory of life.

Sensuality results. They are escapists from reality. In books they read, in words they heed, in thoughts they entertain, in habits they indulge, in appetites they do not control, they dissipate their manhood or their womanhood.

Impurity results. They trade love for lust, liberty for license, respect for ribaldry, shame for smut, decency for dirt. God offers them a palace of life. They prefer the sty of existence. (But the offer remains.)

Disregard for others results. They reach beyond their needs, and greed creeps in. They make covetousness their creed. They propagate unholy patterns of acquisitiveness. Professional rapacity walks about in respectable clothes—thoughtless of the poverty and suffering of others.

And this is hell. For this is separation from God, from other selves, from our true selves.

O God, forgive us if, through greed and grasping for ourselves, we have not found our place in thy design. O God, forgive us if, in our pride and pleasure, we have been insensible to thee. O Father, restore us to thyself. Amen.

THE CHRIST-HABIT

4:20-21 But it is different with you. You have acquired Christ as a habit of life; you have, that is, if you are attentive to him and are disciplined by him, by the reality of meaning found in Jesus.

It is different with you if Christ is your way through life.

No longer do your activities ride you through a rat race, your attitudes limit you to local approval, your anxieties smother you in smoldering fears. Christ is your habit, now.

Christ becomes a habit with those who are attentive to him. What gets your attention gets you. What does get your attention? The prurient or the pure? The paltry or the great? The gossip of your fears or the God of your trust? We become like those with whom we wish to identify. We become a bit like Christ when we identify with those who live by the love of God.

Christ becomes a habit with those who are ruled by God's spirit. We could dissipate potentials in human life and let our minds and bodies slip to self-indulgent decay. We can, on the other hand, discipline the possibilities in human life to the control of God's purpose, to the compulsion of his power, to the completion of his presence.

Christ is a habit with those who find their meaning in his meaning. We can find meaning in the words that Jesus taught; they measure human relationships. We can find meaning in the way that Jesus went; it makes a worthwhile goal to go for. We find meaning in the life that Jesus lived; it marks the reality of God in the universe. We find meaning in the death that Jesus died and in his victory in death; it means the triumph of his eternal meaning.

When Christ is the habit of our lives, our thoughts become as prayers, our words become his praise, our homes become his meeting place, our work his creative acts, our lives become his hymns, and our deaths his benedictions.

O God, we look to thee through the message and meaning of Jesus. May Christ, thy love, thy purpose, become the dominating habit of our lives. Amen.

99

CHRIST INSTEAD

4:22 Christ taught you to throw off your old way of life. It was spoiling—all mixed up by your lusts.

Fling off the rotting past!

How can we? Floundering in deep water a man would desperately grasp at any object that might save him from his drowning. Only a suicide, in such a situation, would refuse a lifesaver, a buoy, raft, or strong helping hand to lift him from his peril. Floundering in habits that could destroy his mind or body, who would refuse an offer of help? A drowning man may be too weak to help himself. So may we have been—so mixed up, so worn out, so engulfed.

God helps—if we permit him. His power is greater than our weakness.

Letting him help us begins with recognizing our despair. It begins, too, with desiring a new and vigorous spirit. A man will care for his automobile. Why not his body and his mind? An automobile, neglected, can rust away in its unseen parts. So can man's nature, by the accumulation of lustful impulses, by irreverence for the sacredness of every life. The splendor of life God gave him atrophies. This happens slowly, insidiously, a hidden rot not noticed until it stinks. The stink is moral decay. The seaminess of moral ruin is stamped at last upon his face.

Our lives were spoiling, but we hid this from ourselves. We accepted all the popular delusions that call these sick habits "life." We did until we saw they were the seeds of death.

In the old life sometimes we looked for God. Maybe we even went to church. The clinging rot remained. But now we have confessed our helplessness. He lifts us from our mess. He renews us. God becomes the center of our lives. From his vantage we see the old life was perverted. We turn from all its putridness. We throw it away, renounce it, bury it. New life is never new as long as we look back. New life is ahead.

We see thy Christ, O God, ahead of us. We follow. We turn our backs on the past of our mistakes. We take the life thou dost offer us, renewed by thee, renewed for thee. Amen.

A DAILY RENEWAL

4:23 But now you are to be daily made new in your mental attitude.

You are to be daily renewed in your total outlook on life.

The wick in the old candle burned itself out. The light now turned on is renewed constantly from a source outside itself. So is the new life fed by God's spirit coming to us. Life from him is fresh, clear, strong.

These are the processes into the new life:

We are taught, disciplined by God's spirit as we are attentive to him (4:21).

We discard the old ways of life (4:22).

We take on, instead, a new manhood enabled by, and imaging, God's (4:24).

This new life does not grow old. It is God's life among us. Our days come and go, our bodies grow and decay, but the vitality of his life among us remains (II Cor. 4:16).

This new life is a renewal of spirit. Our lives become charged with God's affection for all his creatures.

This new life is a renewal of mind. Our minds become alert to God's purpose in all his creation.

This new life is life in his church. It is Christ—renewed with every generation of God's people.

When our spirits droop, O God, and when our minds grow dull, we draw upon thy spirit, the mind that was in Jesus. Renew us daily. Be thou the spirit that brings us, thy church, to new and vital life in the world. Amen.

A NEW PERSON

4:24 *Be the new person God created you to be, living an upright life, a life of wholesome integrity and responsibility to God.*

You are a new person.

You were, at any rate, created to be a new person. Like a larva created to be a winged creature! Within the cocoon the larva changed into a pupa with a built-in power to break out of the cocoon and emerge as a new adult. Some larvae never make it. They die or are devoured. Too many men and women never make it beyond mental and social adolescence, never put on garments of maturity.

This year's tree is last year's. But with springtime it was clothed with new, fresh leaves. Last year's leaves are dead. It is a human embarrassment to see curled up, dried up attitudes of childishness still clinging to supposed adults. God intended us to grow. We can grow new attitudes and a new likeness to God. We can. God intended it so. Slip on this new person-hood. Equip yourself with God-quickened vitality. Sheathe yourself with his person—with Christ. For Christ cannot remain objective. He is God's trace among men moving onward through our times. Keep current with him. Keep alive with the renewed life of him.

This new life is the imaging of God. It is the imitating of Christ. It is to live as he would live. Sincerely, single-mindedly do the work God places in your hand, responsible to him, a new person responding to God's person.

As we, his church, live in the spirit of Christ, we become God's community among men.

> *"Dear Lord and Father of mankind,*
> *Forgive our foolish ways;*
> *Reclothe us in our rightful mind,*
> *In purer lives thy service find,*
> *In deeper reverence, praise." Amen.*[11]

A NEW RELATIONSHIP

4:25 Having stripped falseness away then, speak truth each with the next man, because we belong to one another as the parts of one body.

We are new persons in a transparent relationship with one another.

We are new persons because we belong to one Person, Christ. We are parts of his body, the church. We live, that is, in a new personhood with one another in God's family.

In the family of God there is nothing to hide. The ancient Zoroastrians likened God to light and fire. He was the enemy of falseness which to them epitomized all evil. His fire could burn it away. Love does that. Love, remember, is the bond of God's family. Falseness is the front fear puts up between individuals by which they try to hide from one another. Love burns fear and melts the barriers. We used to fight this love. It frightened us. The brightness of God's love showed us up, unhid, before all eyes. This exposure embarrassed us; it was strange to us at first. But this is the way it is among the members of God's family. They've nothing to hide.

In the family of God we have everything to show. There is *self*-evidence: an openness of life among us. There is sincerity: a truthfulness of speech among us. There is simplicity: an artlessness of manner. There is sharing: a considerateness for each other. The scientist George Washington Carver, who turned his genius to build a food economy for the poor, was known for his simplicity. It was a mark of his singleness of purpose: his artless love for all God's creatures and so for all his fellow men.

We are to live as though we belonged to one another. We do if we are parts of Christ's body. We share with each other our highest impulses and thoughts.

Father, make us clean, make our lives clear. Tear away false fronts. Give us the courage of thy love to live transparently, simply, and sincerely with the members of thy household. Teach us to be true to all. Amen.

A NEW FEEL

4:26 Be indignant at wrongdoing, and do not do wrong yourself. Do not let any day come to an end with you still fuming in exasperation.

No longer feel for yourselves. Feel for others.

Be indignant, now, at indignities to others. In the old life you became angry at those who crossed you. In the new life you may be angry at any act or custom, habit or policy that disrespects a human person or disregards his health and wholeness.

Abhor wrongdoing so much that you would not do wrong yourself. You despise the old wrongs you used to do if your life is truly new. Beware, however, lest in despising wrong, you despise wrongdoers. They are as worthy as you to find new life. Antagonism even to evil can be evil as well if it becomes ill will to evildoers. South Indian people say: "Anger is a stone cast into a nest of wasps."

You must beware of lingering exasperation. Exasperation, nursed, becomes a grudge that wears the mind and tears the body. Never go to bed at night until you know you are at peace—in love with God and man.

For love, Paul wrote, is not easily provoked. Pedro used to be easily provoked. A colorful bandit of the Argentine pampas, he had a reputation for his flaming temper and his deadly knife. But when he accepted the meaning of Christ, his violence was transformed. His passion changed to compassion, his flaming temper to tenderness for fellow creatures who had been wronged. He was still a colorful, rugged person, but Christ's person.

Father, the day begins with thee. Let it end with thee. And let the hours between fill our minds and hearts with attitudes of love. Let love be full of angry judgment at wrong to human life. Let love be fully forgiving toward wronged and wrongdoer for thy sake. Amen.

OVERCOMING WITH GOOD

4:27 Don't give the devil a chance at you.

Don't give a slanderer an occasion to point the finger at you.

Don't give wrong an opportunity to get back on top of you.

This phrase the letter writer inserted between two dangers. They are dangers that want to get into the act when we fill our new role as people of God.

One is the danger of using evil in our enmity to evil. Hatred can never destroy hatred. Violence cannot prevent violence for long. Mistrust does not create trust. To champion the church by rousing suspicion and anger against evildoers may make us unwitting tools of evil. God needs no defense, least of all by methods opposite his character of justice and mercy.

Boris Pasternak once wrote in *Dr. Zhivago:* "If the beast who sleeps in man could be held down by threats—any kind of threat, whether of jail or of retribution after death—then the highest emblem of humanity would be the lion tamer in the circus with his whip, not the prophet who sacrificed himself. But don't you see, this is just the point—what has for centuries raised man above the beast is not the cudgel but an inward music: the irresistible power of unarmed truth, the powerful attraction of its example."

There is the danger of losing goodness through the failure to use goodness. Truth must be lived. It is just as wrong not to do right as it is to do wrong.

Don't give the devil even a place to sit among you!

Take over, God, from the satyr and the saint who struggle in our hearts. Our human goodness is such a shady counterpart of human wrong. Arrest this tiring sport among us and put us to work in the factory of thy perfect love. Amen.

OVERCOMING WITH WORK

4:28 Any one of you for whom pilfering has been a habit must no longer take anything not his. Instead, he should work hard, engage himself in useful work with his own hands so that he has enough to share with those in need.

The joy of hard work fits us for the joy of sharing the fruit of our labor.

But some of us have pilfered. We have pilfered little things from the office, perhaps. We have pilfered a fellow worker's good name in little words we have said in gossip. We have pilfered the time of others, lazy at their expense. We have stolen from the common wealth when we have received wages for wasted hours or shoddy workmanship. We have stolen from the poor and weak when we have profited on their distress. It is thievery to misuse others to contrive ease and position. It is thievery to refuse community responsibility. It is thievery to find ways to get rich quick and to live luxuriously. It is thievery to use our talents, our intellect, our diligence purely for selfish gain.

Now learn the joy of hard work. "Good living" in this letter writer's counsel is not lesiure. For him the good life is working so hard that by nightfall you are weary, ready for renewing sleep. For work he used a word that means "grow weary" and another word that signifies the manual labor of farmhands, of slaves, of quarrymen and miners. Charles Kingsley wrote: "Being forced to work, and forced to do your best, will breed in you . . . a hundred virtues which the idle never know."

Now learn the joy of sharing. Sharing is giving what we have sweated to earn. What we do not share becomes too heavy a burden for any of God's children to bear. Talent is a gift. Diligence to apply oneself is a gift. God gives these gifts not for our own enrichment. They are trusts given us to invest for the sake of others.

We thank thee, God, for the gift of hard work. Teach us to work for thee and to share the fruit of our work with the least of these, our brothers. Amen.

OVERCOMING WITH WORDS

4:29 Don't let any foul language come out of your mouths. But do speak the good word that is suitable for the occasion— helpful words to others, words that build the morale and the spirit of the church.

Words can destroy, but words can also build.

Words can destroy. In quarrel they can incite to destructive passion. They can be acrimonious, spiteful (Jas. 3:8-9). They can discourage their hearers. They may be used as a cloak to hide behind. Some people to whom the letter writer writes, like some of us, had the habit of using dirty language. Foul language is the stink of putrefaction in little minds. They stench the soundwaves. They are a miasma that smothers the fresh vigor of human thought.

Words can be empty. Many, like the people in Anton Chekhov's plays, talk of themselves and do not really listen to other *persons*, listen only superficially to the words the other persons say. What others say only remind them of themselves.

But words can build. Words can nourish the mind and strengthen the spirit. Such words are not spoken lightly. India's Gautama (the Buddha) feared that frivolous language disturbed the mind from the truth. China's Mo Ti warned that words should not be spoken except when they carry good counsel. The Greek Pythagoras advised silence except when words are worth more than silence. The letterwriter says: Speech among God's people should be to the point, helpful words thoughtfully spoken. Speak words that affirm your hearers as persons you respect, words that flood the soundwaves with goodwill, that build the fellowship in faith.

"Let the words of my mouth and the meditation of my heart
   be acceptable in thy sight,
  O Lord, my rock and my redeemer." Amen.

(Ps. 19:14 RSV)

GOD'S SPIRIT AMONG US

4:30 *Also, be careful not to cross God's guiding spirit, his presence among you. His spirit has marked you as the people who belong to God's future, to the time when all will be restored to him and you will be fully free in him.*

Be alert to God's spirit, and behave as his people.

Are we his people? What indications are there? How can we, or anyone else, know?

You know there is a wind when it blows. You feel it on your face. You see its moving effect through the trees, the grasses. Well, we are brothers of the wind of God. God blows through our lives.

Do not fight the wind of God. Do not set yourself against his current among us. Do not run counter to his guidance. A devout missionary lady, at prayer, felt moved with love for everyone. But an old bitterness in her life made her tongue caustic and her heart at hate with all who did not believe her creed. Thus she denied the very God she professed. Her life ran counter to his leading.

A man went to a highly advertised discount store. He found the goods shoddy. He said he would like to have a warning sign in front of the store: "No value here!" A world of people hungry for value have put an imaginary sign in front of many a church building: "No value here!" Do we live outside the church as though God did not exist? We are responsible for secularism, for social immorality, for philosophies of despair, when we have crossed God's guiding spirit.

We have tried to identify God with ourselves. We are meant to identify ourselves with God. God's action among us should be our identity. They who really belong to God live in his presence now. They do not wait for some cataclysmic breakthrough to bring redemption. They live redemptively now. The world will see in us the harmony of God's perfect society only if we are truly his.

God, we realize we are not really thine if all we have is thy name. Let our fellowship of faith be marked by thy spirit. Free us from our separate selfishness and use our unity of love to restore thy creation to thyself. Amen.

THE SPIRIT OF GOD'S PEOPLE

4:31 Now that you are a new people of God, let there be no trace of bitterness or of any strong passion or anger.

God's people can remain together as God's people because the rough edges of self-centered emotion drop from their lives.

Among us there can be no rancor. Where there is love there is no bitter spirit, no bitter word. Bitterness festers in self-pity. It fosters ill will. It focuses on felt injuries. Its language is harsh, acrimonious. But we—if we live now for God's time —we are too interested in others to nurse any rankling hurt to ourselves.

Among us there can be no rage. Rage may be the outburst of a revengeful spirit. It is a geyser of scalding hate that gushes from a person who can no longer keep it suppressed. It rushes, a destructive flood, through all his mind, putting reason out of order. It is reckless of friend and fellow man. It is the vibration of taut self-sensitivity. He is a weakling, whoever is subject to his tempers. He is a slave whomever passion rules. But we—if we live now for God's time—we carry no chips on our shoulders. We have no conceit to be outraged, no pent-up feelings that need escape.

Among us there is no resentment. Resentment may be a paranoid response to circumstance. It is a reaction to irritation without control and without concern for others. It is a brooding disregard for their needs. But we—if we live now for God's time—we have a consideration for others deep enough to channel our emotions. We care more for the wholeness of society than for the contentment of ourselves.

God's purpose is to bring about the time when all will be liberated from destructive emotions. To the extent we are free from them, we belong to that time.

Father, may we live in the spirit of thy people. Swallow up our passions in thy compassion. Amen.

THE WAY OF GOD'S PEOPLE

4:31 Now that you are a new people of God, let there be no trace . . . of any clamor and insults or of any kind of ill will.

God's people can remain together as God's people because the rough edges of self-centered emotions drop from their lives.

Among us there is no rioting. Rioting is the clamor of those whose need, or fear, is more important to them at the moment than anything else. It is the mood of the screaming, shrieking child not yet old enough to know that other people are as important as he. Some never grow beyond this stage in social morality. They clamor for what they want—attention and more care. "Give me mine!" they cry. "Notice me!" But we—if we live now for God's time—we recognize the equal importance of others and care about their needs. We bear one another's burdens patiently.

Among us there is no railing. A quarreling church profanes the house of God with a godless racket. Insults, direct or implied, are insults to the creator of all human beings. When anyone defames, or entertains a defamation of his fellow men, he mocks God's call for unity in love. But we—if we live now for God's time—we think and speak goodwill to one another. We look for the best in each other. We honor one another.

Among the people of God there can be no ill will at all. The faults the letter writer lists are faults of those who cannot really see others because they are blinded by themselves. Their edges are sharp. They cut one another. But we—if we live for God's time—we have our edges bent to link with one another like linked mail.

God's purpose is to bring about the time when all will be liberated from destructive emotions. To the extent we are free from them, we belong to that time.

Father, may we walk in the way of thy people. Share with us, that we may share with one another, thy patience and thy goodwill. Amen.

110

THE KINDNESS OF GOD'S PEOPLE

4:32 Rather, be kind to one another.

God's people are joined by God's attitudes among them.

God's people are kind. Kindness is the golden chain that binds the world together. God's love binds us. With his love we love. They who know they belong to Christ accept every other person, no matter what he is, or who he is, or where he is. That is how God accepts *us*.

God's people are kind. In Cloverbottom's riverside community "being saved" meant an annual emotional explosion little related to life the rest of the year. Then Luther Davis was "saved." For him that meant giving himself, his family, and everything he did, to God. He taught himself to read the New Testament, and then he lived by it. It led him to attitudes of openness and kindness toward his neighbors. All year they could count on him. Christ became the atmosphere of his home.

God's people are kind. True kindness is God's goodness acting through us. True kindness is no occasional good turn, but a character of daily life whereby others know they can, at any time, in any place, rely on us and come to us for understanding. True kindness is trueheartedness, wholeheartedness. Rich food tastes good, but can also make one ill. Nourishing food is always wholesome. A kind person is a wholesome person to have around.

Father, it is good to be with thee in life and to be with all the people who are with thee. Keep us kind, open-minded, openhearted. Thou hast accepted us. Like thee, we would accept all others. Amen.

THE ATTITUDES OF GOD'S PEOPLE

4:32 . . . *Tenderhearted, forgiving, as God in Christ forgives you.*

God's people are joined by God's attitudes among them.

God's people are tenderhearted. Tenderheartedness is awareness of God's creatures and sensitivity to their needs. It is born of strength, not sentiment. It is the courage to care. It is never hurried; the hurried pass need by on the other side. It is never worried; the worried look the other way from need.

God's people are tenderhearted. Tenderheartedness is compassion. Passion, uncontrolled, can sicken the entire body and mind. Compassion can bind the wounds of others (and heal, in the process, one's own wounds).

God's people are forgiving. Forgiveness is an act of a generous, gracious nature. So forgiveness is also an attitude. Admiration accepts others for their greatness. Forgiveness accepts others for themselves—even when their faults and flaws show through. Forgiveness never closes the door on anyone who closes his own door in deception, or on anyone who locks his own door in antagonism. He who forgives nurtures no dislike for one who has wronged him. He does not shun him, nor cut him off. Forgiveness, true, must be received to be meaningful for him who is forgiven. But it does not have to be received to be meaningful to him who forgives; for forgiveness, when it comes, remains constantly open, constantly acceptant.

God's people are forgiving. Forgiveness for one another grows out of God's forgiveness for us. If God, like Christ, can love such unlikely things as we, we can love any others—all others. We share with all his generosity to us. Who loves not others loses himself as well as others. Who belongs to God belongs to everyone.

Now these are plural qualities. No one is kind, tenderhearted, forgiving by himself. We live for one another, and others live by us. For we all live in God.

Our Father, forgive us that we may forgive others. We receive thy love that we may love as thou dost love. Amen.

112

IMITATE GOD

5:1 *As children, then, secure in their father's love, become God's imitators.*

God is portrayed by his people.

God owns us, loves each of us as a good father loves his only child. Children imitate their parents. They want to be like those they admire. They live in imaginative earnestness the adult world toward which they are growing. God's children imitate him—his love, his forgiveness, his purity. We copy the life toward which we are growing. God our Father is one, and we are his together in his church. He brought us together. In our unity we bear the family likeness.

There is no family likeness in imitation religion. A posed religion is shallow. It is a thin portrait over a painting of lust and violence. It were better to side with atheists who will not believe the mimic God we too often have projected on the world screen. We should reject the caricature of God our divisive tribal religion too often images. Instead, we should practice to be like him whom Jesus knew as Father.

If we are God's children we will imitate him. To reject God is to try to put oneself in God's place. To accept Christ's God is to try to be like God. We become like that which we imitate. When Jesus called Judas "son of perdition" (John 17:12), he indicated that the qualities of lostness were prominent in Judas. When their colleagues called James and John the "sons of thunder" (Mark 3:17), they described their tempers of vehemence. To be called sons and daughters of God means that our lives remind men of God's qualities. The character of civilizations is molded by the people's imitation of leading persons. People pattern themselves after strong leaders. God's people pattern their lives after God alone.

We can imitate the practices of our times that pressure us to conform us. Or we can imitate God, who inspires us to transform us.

Our Father, we want to become like thee in love, in forgivingness, and in clean discipline. Help us represent thy greatness in our daily lives. Amen.

LIVE GOD'S LOVE

5:2 *Lead loving lives in the way Christ loved you and completely gave himself for you. This is the good way to worship God.*

True worship is to live the love with which God loves.

Worship has too often been to a self-projected image of God. Who has not liked gifts and been persuaded by them? So men have thought they could bribe God with gifts. Man likes food and pleasant smells. So men in earlier days have burned their best food on altars to please God with the smell of it. Man likes to be admired. So men have thought God would like great honor, and they have praised him. Modern man, in our society of individuals, wants his neighbor to behave himself and not intrude on his private affairs. So modern men suspect that God is pleased when men behave themselves and do not intrude on God's distant privacy.

None of these pleases God. The fact is, God does not stand around waiting to be pleased. He loves. He does not ask to be served for himself. He acts. He is not a receiving God. He gives. He gives himself.

Jesus said again and again that man should give himself. To give self as Christ did is to turn oneself completely to love anyone in need. Everyone is in need of God's love to complete his life. Creation needs God's love to complete its meaning.

This completeness is his purpose. It is his persistent, penetrating purpose. It has no time for dallying. We are to stop dallying with religion and to lead our daily lives in self-committed love. Then we will understand what it is to be like God and to be with God, that "the whole purpose for which we exist is to be thus taken into the life of God." [1]

Walk to and fro through life with love.

Forgive us, God, that too often our service in thy name has been contrived to safeguard ourselves, our tradition, and our institutions. Help us as thy church to give ourselves completely up to love the world that needs thy love. Amen.

NO ROOM FOR WRONG

5:3 *And because you are God's consecrated people it is right that among you there should not be even a suggestion of sexual promiscuity, of dirty words of any kind, or any greedy disregard for the rights of others.*

The behavior of God's people is becoming to Christ.

A dress is "becoming" when it suits the person wearing it, emphasizing her beauty. People often indicate their school, club, or religious affiliation by some symbol that they wear. The followers of Christ show their association with him by doing nothing that would not become him.

God made our bodies to be used well, not abused. Irregular sexual practice is abuse not only of our bodies but of mental integrity and emotional security. It is an abuse of trust, of fellowship, of respect, of all the things that make for the unity God purposes in Christ. It puts the physical self and the moment's personal gratification above the other person and above other persons and so above God.

God made our minds to be filled with health, not filth. The more we clutter them with dirt, the less easily can we apprehend beauty and truth. Like a car speeding down the highway with its windshield spattered, we speed through life, vision blurred. Spatterings of coarse conversation, salacious lies, all sights and all sounds that divert the mind from what is wholesome, uplifting, and good are dirty. Dirty minds become deranged from mental alertness to real values.

God gave us people to esteem, not to slander. Who plunders people? The worst plunderers are those who use people for their own profit or pleasure. Lust plunders another's body. Cupidity plunders another's mind. Rapacity plunders another's bread. The prejudice of pride plunders another's human dignity.

God's people are consecrated to him. Consecration means to give oneself with all one's heart to carry out God's purpose.

Make us so bold for thee, O God, that we will strip all that is unlike thee from every conversation, from every practice and profession, from every trade and traffic in which we engage. Amen.

REGARD FOR OTHERS

5:3 . . . Or any greedy disregard for the rights of others.

The behavior of God's people is becoming to Christ.

"A city set on a hill," Jesus once said, "cannot be hid." No more can we when we profess to follow him. "Let your light so shine before men," he said (Matt. 5:14b, 16a RSV). We represent God in the world. Therefore we do not do (surely should not do) the things he would not do.

Nathan went to David with a story of a rich man stealing a poor man's sheep (II Sam. 12:1-6). David was indignant at the rich man. Nathan said, "You are the man!" Might a Nathan say today, "You are the man, you who write lewd books by which adults lose their sense of human values, who portray violence by which children lose their sense of human sympathy, who benefit from systems whereby the sick are burdened with debt and the poor are deprived of legal justice, who demand high wages for careless labor whereby the consumer loses dependable workmanship, who seek high profits whereby the customer loses quality, who distort the news whereby the reader loses truth, who tempt and excite human desires for your wares whereby the public loses the high virtues of thrift and frugality, who waste the purse of commonwealth whereby the citizens lose value for their taxes, who coax men to borrow and lend to them at usury!" We who live in our pleasant houses in an age of homeless men, who eat excessively in a world of hungry men, who dress expensively when millions have only a ragged garment to wear, who make our income the standard of success when humanity's greatest need is a standard of honesty—are we the men? Jesus said, "He who has two coats, let him share with him who has none" (Luke 3:11 RSV).

God's people are to do what God would do among them.

You are our God, O God of justice and of love! We are the men you made to serve, to be just, to love our fellow men. As you regard us, so may we regard others. Amen.

GRATEFUL CONVERSATION

5:4 Nor should there be any indecency, inane or facetious talk among you. That is in bad taste. Instead, your conversation should be in a mood of gratefulness.

No one with good sense would clutter a castle with debris. No one, in the clean goodness of God's presence, likes conversation or actions that are disorderly.

When friends who have delightful experiences to tell about meet each other, they do not pass their time in bored, empty-headed talk. Their common interests are shared. They learn from one another.

When companions work together on a research project or in creative artwork, they have no time to kill. When they exchange information, they do not dawdle with the idle. When they share appreciation for the beautiful they do not dabble with the ugly.

In the fellowship of Christ we have great thoughts to share. We have a common purpose to pursue, cooperative tasks to work creatively. We appreciate the beautiful God has given us. Just as a bad odor does not belong in a kitchen, nor a dead plant in a flowerpot, nor rotting food in the pantry; just so malodorous, decadent, rotten words and thoughts have no place among God's people. Anything that spoils the atmosphere, spoils the growth, spoils the nourishment of Godlike fellowship is out of place.

In this fellowship we simply do not enjoy the stench of indecency. We find no pleasure in indecent stories and pictures. We simply do not enjoy the stupidity of foolish talk or conversation that evades stimulants to the mind and inspiration to the spirit.

For us life is a grateful thing. We are grateful for God's presence and for God's people. We are grateful for a goal in life that stretches beyond time, and grateful for gaiety in life that reaches beyond tears.

Father, may the reminders each day brings of thy gracious love fill us with gratitude and crowd out all worthless words and thoughts from among us. Amen.

OUTSIDE GOD'S COMPANY

5:5 For you can be sure of this: no one who is sexually promiscuous or filthy-minded, or who takes advantage of others to gratify himself (all these are ways of setting oneself in the place of God) has any part in the inheritance of God's and Christ's community.

We know that faith is relevant to life.

We know that princes do not live in pigsties, nor pigs in palaces. If we have become a part of the people of God, we know that lust and indecency and self-seeking have no place among them.

The writer is not warning us to be good for reward in the sweet by-and-by. He is reminding us that we cannot know the presence of God and continue the practices of wrongdoing. Here is no external commandment to be holy, but an internal compunction to be whole. If we are the people of God, we know what it is to act like God's people.

Outside God's company are all the sexually promiscuous, the sensually prurient, the selfishly pretentious. They have no respect for other persons, no reverence for God, no regard for themselves.

Sexual promiscuity is lack of respect for others as persons. Sensual prurience is lack of reverence for God as Father. Selfish pretention is lack of regard for oneself as a son of God. These practices make an idol of the self, superceding God. Every practice that defrauds another has no place in God's company, for it violates all that characterizes God.

Christ characterizes God. We characterize his community if we are really in it.

O Spirit of God, lead us away from all that is contrary to the heritage of thy clean goodness to which thou callest us. Amen.

THE ANGER OF LOVE

5:6 Do not let anyone deceive you with shallow theories. These are the practices of those who ignore God and thereby incur the anger of God.

Treat life badly, and life is bad for you.

Let no one deceive you with fancy theories. Down does not lead up. Southward does not lead northward. Ignoring God does not teach us to know God. Stubborn selfishness does not mature us to unselfishness. Disobedience to God's purpose does not prepare us for participation in his plans. Spurning his presence does not assure us his future. Hate does not fructify in love. Sin does not evolve into purity. Let no one deceive you. Faith in God fits us for this life. Without responsible human relationships creeds are hollow words.

But does God show anger? Man's anger is his hate. Hate is the child of his hurt ego. God's anger is his love. Love never ceases to love. Love permits love's object to refuse love. *This* is love's anger—that, permitting such refusal, it presses still its love on him who refuses love. He who refuses love cannot escape his consciousness of refusal. He runs from love, plunges more deeply into the deeds that scoff at love—into sexual promiscuity, foulness of speech, the chase after material gain. He flings himself outside God's plan.

This is God's anger—his disposition against all that separates from him those whom he loves. His anger is his pain that burns around our separateness from him. Until we feel his pain and enter into his pain for us, we cannot enter his plans for us.

God's anger is his pressure on the vacuum in our lives where he should be. It is love's impact on unlove. God's anger is his affirmation of us in our denial of him. God's anger is his blow to our self-image. His forgiveness deflates our self-importance.

Love is not indulgent of unlove. God is not sentimental about the Godless.

O God, who never turns away from us, restore us from our neglect of thee by the anger of thy love. Unite our faith in thee to our behavior in society. Amen.

CAUGHT IN OUR CHOICES

5:7 So do not become caught up in their doings.

"Every man is like the company he is wont to keep." [2]

If we take part in activities that leave God out, we leave ourselves out of any conscious part in God's activity.

God's invitation, which this letter carries, is to become a part of God's company. This is fellowship that works for God's tomorrow. This is the group that moves together in the direction of God's purpose. If we are a part of God's company, we work, we move, together with his company.

If we stay behind, we remain a part of the company that stays behind. Our desire to belong to the people about us may incline us to do what they do. We may go along with habits which indulge the ego and the appetites. The basic cowardice of wrongdoing is its hiding in the crowd, its fear to step out and follow right. We may run with the crowd, but the crowd runs around a lonely center. The crowd may be an aggregate of isolated individuals. Togetherness may be based on common activities or interests in which each individual looks for personal satisfaction by feeding on the other. Jackals run in packs for the sake of each jackal's hunger. But when one jackal sickens, the others attack him. The company that loves sin hates the sinner when he is broken by his sin.

The company that loves God hates sin but loves the sinner and wants to bring him to the fellowship of God's people. The company of God serves one another's needs, bears one another's burdens.

If we keep company with those who love God with his love we become like them—like the members of God's family.

We have to make a choice: either the company of those who leave God or the company of those who love God.

Father, help us make the choice. Firmly fix us in thy company to become what thou wouldst have us be. Amen.

120

ENLIGHTENED LIVES

5:8 Your lives were once as dark as darkness, but now, in your Master's company your lives are as light as the light. So conduct yourselves as enlightened people.

When you make a choice you make a step from "then" to "now."

The "then" of a life lived in the company of those who ignore God is described as darkness. The darkness describes the life of him who does not know where he is, or where he is going. The "now" of life in the company of God's people is described as "light."

C. S. Lewis once described those who live for themselves as inhabitants of a city in the dusk of imminent night. He described those who live for God as inhabitants of a land in the dawn of imminent day. The difference is between the end and the beginning.

The "end" nature of existence is isolation from others, lost in the dark outside. The "beginning" nature of life is a gathering with others in the light, inside, in God's presence. Cursing outside. Conversation inside. Grumbling outside, and stumbling when one tries to walk, fumbling when one tries to help another. The people inside have no better eyes than those outside, but they can see—they have the light to see by. The people inside have no better hands than those outside, but they can help—they have a light to work by. Those inside cannot hide. Those outside can. They have the dark to hide in. Those inside do not want to hide. Fellowship in light is better than loneliness in the dark.

Here is the difference between frustration and freedom, between dead-end lives and open-highway lives. The difference is not between inherent badness and inherent goodness, the difference is in the locus of life. A life in God's atmosphere lives, in ego's miasma dies. Christ has illumined for us life's meaning—a meaning we can live by, a way we can walk in.

By the light of his standard we conduct our lives.

We are grateful, Father. We were suspended in the dark between vast uncertainties, but by Christ we have seen light, and certainty has found us. Amen.

121

LIGHT GOD LENDS

5:9 *Enlightenment shows itself in wholehearted goodness, rightness, trueness.*

Gems possessing luster are not seen in the dark, only in the light.

Inside God's household the light is on. It spots our spottiness, but it also stimulates our possibilities. His light, which "darkness cannot dispel," burns up our trash, brings out our trust so that together, as God's people, we can wholeheartedly express his goodness, his rightness, his trueness.

Goodness is the multiplication of God's action among us as we act his goodness toward one another. Rightness is the quality of our desire and deeds in applying God's will, his plan, to all of life. Trueness is our sincere surrender to God's meaning.

Goodness is kindness. It is both the spontaneous response to God's goodness and the spontaneous reaction of delight in people. It honors God at the same time that it helps people. It is well-doing that comes from the sense of well-being as God's children.

Rightness is justice. It is the characteristic of those who have been put right by God. It is both reverence for God and respect for his creatures. It is dutiful to God in the obedience of sons to their father. It is dutiful to man in the considerateness of brothers to their brothers. It is the quality of a well-ordered life, well-balanced living.

Trueness is depth and solidity. A travesty for truth among individuals and nations is the rationalization of self-interest. Truth needs no excuses. It stands starkly clear for what it is. It cannot escape notice. It conceals nothing. The opposite of display and dreams, it is deeds, the genuine in action. Trueness is courageous, defenseless confrontation of our lives and of our world with God.

Give us a light, please, God, so we can get out of our murky-minded past. Give us thy sunlight to nourish our lives that we may live thy goodness, do thy rightness, think thy trueness day by day. Amen.

TEST IT

5:10 *Make sure what it is that squares with God.*

The people of God want to find out what fits in with the character of God.

One puts fine print under the light to read it. One brings a fabric into the natural light to examine its true color. The people of God test their thoughts, their attitudes, and their actions by the light of him who makes life. This must be the continuing concern of the church. For each situation and each generation plans and programs must be tested, renewed, adapted, as God's spirit leads us.

The father who wishes the best for his children plans well for them while permitting choices, decisions, creative expression by his children. Thus, God plans for us. By consulting God's plans we become conformable to his nature—"like father, like son." The more sensitive we are to his counsel, the more clearly we discern the genuineness of a God-directed life.

The owner of a new hi-fi set which he himself has put together is eager to test it to see how it works. We prove the plan of God by letting him put us together and finding out how we work. Whatever stands up under strain, whatever endures through difficulties, proves itself. And we examine ourselves to note what in us measures up to the maturity God expects of us.

Yes, God does accept us as we are. But then we, to be with him, must accept his purpose in our lives.

We examine ourselves to see what it is that can measure up to the maturity God expects of us.

O God, let our lives square with thy purpose for us. O God, rule our lives. Transform us from ourselves to be conformed to thee. Help us distinguish thy will from our willfulness. Amen.

LEAVE THE DARK

5:11 *Quit associating yourselves with useless activities of a shady character. Instead, expose them.*

Time, toil, talent—these tools are given us to help us do our part in God's plan. Don't waste them.

Jesus told a parable of the fruitless fig tree. Bearing no fruit, it took up precious space, so it was ordered cut down and burned (Luke 13:6-9). The useless life has no place in God's plan.

The letter writer is saying here, "You have been associating yourself, you know, with activities that are questionable in character, activities about which you really cannot be above-board when you come face to face with God and truth. So quit them."

A salesman followed his company's pattern of soliciting prospective customers with nightclub entertainment, with drinks, lavish meals, and shows. Results were occasional business contracts, but at the expense of basic integrity. It was a form of bribery, a failure of stewardship in expenses. He quit.

We are here for a great purpose, and we have no right to waste our lives on lesser goals. We have results to produce for God.

As speed shows up slowness, as accomplishment shows up laziness, we expose uselessness by usefulness. A disciplined, resourceful life shows up the undisciplined, aimless life in the fruit it bears.

Whatever God would have us do, he gives us the ability to do it. He gives us time to do it. We are in his hands. So is our toil. He can take our brief times and toils and talents and work their consequents into the warp and woof of his design. Joined to God, our lives quite naturally bear fruit. Cut off, they cannot (John 15:1-2).

Father, create creativity in our lives for thee. Inspire our industry to use for thy purpose the materials we find at hand. Thus may we communicate thy meaning in new forms of beauty and in new illustrations of goodness. Amen.

DON'T TALK ABOUT IT

5:12 *For it is degrading even to talk about the things that go on among them secretly.*

Christ's followers do not talk about degrading things that others do.

Secret practices still take place behind closed doors and under cover of darkness. We do not know the rites abnormal fringe groups carry on—perhaps fierce group discipline and schemes and rituals of hate. Others, like "mystery religions" of the letter writer's day, gather for their libertine activities— their manhood and womanhood abandoned to narcotic limbo, to sexual deviations, to indiscipline of thought and word, to disorder, or to twisted philosophies.

If we do not know their secret activities, neither do we grasp, avidly, at reports, surmises, and gossip about them. Enjoyment of these things even by hearsay and secondhand discussion is part of the past we've buried. Neither can we repeat "dirt" to someone else without becoming soiled ourselves.

Meantime, are we aboveboard in all our dealings? Or do we Adam-and-Eve-like try to conceal our conscious wrong from God, to hide what we will not share and what we wish to keep secret to ourselves and to our favored groups? Christ's followers have nothing to hide, nothing to defend. They share everything in the open, for all they own is God's.

Dear Father, we would talk among ourselves of the goodness in life. Yet, let us never lose concern for those who have no share in it. Meanwhile, keep us openhearted to all that is true and wholesome. Amen.

5:13 But everything which is exposed to the light is clearly seen for what it is, and what is clearly seen is reflection of the light.

Confronted by God, our lives not only show our evil, but reflect his good.

This double action is important to us. First, the light of God exposes hidden wrong and shows it up for the unpleasantness it is. God holds up our false respectability to scrutiny until we squirm in our exposure.

Second, however, God's light can also be reflected in our lives. On the night of full moon you can read a newspaper by moonlight. Yet the moon is not the origin of its own light. For the sunlight strikes it, shows up its configurations, but also makes of it a light reflecting the light of the sun. Such is the action of God upon our lives. He reveals the smallest ungodliness among us and within us. At the same time he reflects from us his light. The love that exposes us expands itself from us.

Old Bo was an alcoholic. His life was marred before he heard of God's love and accepted the mastery of Christ in his life. His face, although disfigured by past dissipation, now became for many of the neighborhood where he worked the only sign of love they had ever seen. To him they turned for guidance and gladness. This is what Jesus spoke of when he said, "You are the light of the world" (Matt. 5:14 RSV). Our light is his. We shine not for ourselves but for him, that men may see themselves in his light.

Not only is light antipathetic to darkness, it is antiseptic to disease that breeds in darkness. The sunlight destroys germs in the soils of tropical countries. Thus does God's light purify the lives it touches.

Even the mud puddle, Lord, reflects the light of the setting sun, and the beauty of the skies. Even our lives, Lord, light up at thy greatness. Expose to destroy our ugliness, but most of all, let us become a reflection of thy love. Amen.

TURN TOWARD LIGHT

5:14 *There is a saying about this:*
Wake up, sleeper,
And rise up from among the dead,
And Christ will shine upon you.

This is the hymn of new life: "Wake up and live!"

It may have been sung when anyone came up from the water at his baptism. The company on the bank thus joyfully welcomed the new arrival into the day of God for which they lived. It is a good welcome. What if the blankets are warm, and we are snug?

How long will you lie there, O sluggard?
When will you rise from your sleep? (Prov. 6:9 RSV)

Unless you rise you will not see the morning sun. It is good to get up early in the morning to greet the day with song, to fill the day with work.

Even more important is it to get up out of deadly existence—up out of the sedative comfort of a monotonous daily routine. It is good to greet life with song, to work with God's eternal purpose through life. The warmth, the sparkling of Christ, God's full meaning, revitalizes every act and outlook with adventure and assurance.

Like the moon that brightens the night by the light of the sun! So can we lighten the night with Christ who fills the universe. Sri Chakravarti, doing his Brahmin priestly duties in a Hindu temple, found a Gospel and read it. He said the meaning of God which he saw in Christ burst like the sun upon him. He responded to that light, rose to it. "It was like stepping from the dead to life," he said.

Christ is the sunlight of our lives.

Arise, shine, for your light has come.
And the glory of the Lord has risen upon you. (Isa. 60:1 RSV)

"*Sun of my soul, thou Savior dear,*
It is not night if thou be near:
O may no earthborn cloud arise
To hide thee from thy servant's eyes." Amen.[3]

DISCIPLINED LIVING

5:15 See to it, then, that your lives are disciplined, as people sensible to value, not senseless.

Now that we have light through our encounter with God in Christ, we can see, we can live accurately.

God gives us meaning. God gives us purpose. God gives us understanding. When we have risen to the challenge from God, made explicit by Christ, we see what had been vague and meaningless before. We see reason for existence. We find its aim. We sense its value. We feel its joy. We have something to live for. We have something to live by.

We have a map, as it were. We must study the map and watch the road signs. We must look where we are going, do thoughtfully what we do. We need no longer blindly grope our way through religious rite and rote, for we can see our way by him who really is the way. We must be alive to him. We must daily check ourselves by him.

The men and women of God's company are expected to live wisely, accurately. Ask not, then: "Will I gain or suffer for what I am doing?" Ask, rather: "What is God's way of meeting the problem I must meet today? How would Jesus Christ act with the people I will see today?" Think! You have the light of his wisdom to guide you.

"O Lord, . . . direct our minds by thy gracious presence, and watch over our paths with guiding love; that among the snares which lie hidden in the path wherein we walk, we may so press onwards with hearts fixed on thee, that by the track of faith we may come to be where thou wouldest have us; through Jesus Christ our Lord. Amen." [4]

IMMEDIATE LIVING

5:16 Make the most of your time, for these are difficult days.

Your time has come right now—your God-given opportunity to *be*.

You're on! Your role in God's design comes now. These are the days you are accurately to read your lines, to act your part in his purpose. This is no time for fright on the world's stage. Be mature partisans of Christ. You think of all the difficulties in your way? You would be a saint if it were not for . . . ? You would do so much in the church if . . . , but . . . ?

In Jesus' story of the talents, the man who hid his talent for fear and made no use of it received no pity from his master (Matt. 25:14-30).

Yes, these days are difficult. These are troubled days for many when few can see, or seem to care to see, the vivid greatness of God's plan, the growing triumph of his purpose. But you can see. We, his people, can. All the more reason, then, to make the most of time. Here on the hilltop of your faith, here in the clear light of God's love, you have the advantage. Strike now—another time will be too late. This is your time.

This is our time. We see the bargain in the store and snatch it up for it will not be there again. Today! The stranger that passes by! The sorrow of a friend! A struggle in the city! A crisis in the nation! Act now, for God, when you have the opportunity.

But most of all, live now together as God's congregation in mission to the world. Live now as God's persons. Do not let the world cheat you of God's meaning. Be sure you get in life the due measure of reality he offers you. Do not stall. Do not miss the point in life. God gave you these minutes, these hours, these years in history. Fill them.

Let each moment of time be marked with the imprint of eternity.

Because, O God, thou art the creator of what we men call time, and the final solution of all problems, be the counsel of our difficulties; be thou the re-creator of our lives by thine eternity. Amen.

INTELLIGENT LIVING

5:17 *So don't be frantic. Be intelligent about what is the will of God.*

The art of God's people is the art of learning together the sense of his purpose and applying it to life.

To be frantic is to act without good sense. It is the conscious want of sense to meet some crisis—even, perhaps, the crisis of life itself. And who can have good sense if he lives in a world that does not make sense? To live without meaning, without final purpose transcending human struggle and suffering, human hope and import, is to find life senseless. Yet, man longs for ultimate significance, and his unawareness of it in his life situations drives him on his frantic rocking, rolling round.

Generations ago William Cowper wrote:

> Deep in unfathomable mines
> Of never-failing skill
> He treasures up his bright designs,
> And works his sovereign will.
> Blind unbelief is sure to err,
> And scan his work in vain;
> God is his own interpreter
> And he will make it plain.[5]

He does. We can be steady. Life makes sense. Discernment of God's will comes through one another. Not one of us knows all God's plan. But from each other we learn enough to play our part in it, to do his will for us. The congregation of Christ learns to deliberate together in prayerful conversation. We test each other's thoughts. Our thoughts must not be entangled with our egos. God shows parts of his plan to us as we, according to our particular abilities and character, can grasp them. We are expected to chain these parts togther, for God has no will for each of us irrelevant to his will for others.

Father, help us, thy people, listen to thee and to each other and to the world thou dost love: that we may know thy purpose and apply thy will today. Amen.

LIVING ALIVE

5:18 *Don't go drowning yourself in drink. Do not dissipate. Be alive!*

We'll keep the vigor of God for full living!

We are not going to dull our senses and dissipate our time; life is too good for that. To dissipate our time away, to drink away reality—this is not life; this is evasion of life. A free-drinking society is a scared society. Frantic, frightened, frustrated people try to drown their problems and run away from meaning. How many good minds are wasted this way!

> It's monstrous labor, when I wash my brain,
> And it grows fouler.[6]

The letter writer knew of the Dionysian rites, the ecstatic drunken orgies from which some had turned away to follow Christ. He knew their old cronies would be back, urging. He knew. We also know. They come to us and urge us. If not to drinking parties, then to other ways by which the feckless try to find a bit of spice for a rancid life. There are other inebriations. There are intoxications with passion, with pride, and sometimes with power.

The point he makes, repeats, and underlines is this: to follow Christ, to carry out God's will, is a clear decision to permit God's re-creation of a new life within us. We make a clean break. We cannot grasp the rope ladder of a helicopter sent to save us and then let go without falling. We cannot grasp the will of God and then let go without falling back. We must hold on. We can. We are in God's hands.

We need no artificial glee to make life livable, nor inebriation to stupefy us from its encounters. The life which God has given us is good and full and vigorous. They who discover God's will are filled with a living spirit. They are truly alive.

> *"Save us from weak resignation to the evils we deplore;*
> *Let the search for thy salvation be our glory evermore.*
> *Grant us wisdom,*
> *Grant us courage,*
> *Serving thee whom we adore." Amen.*[7]

THE FELLOWSHIP OF GOD'S CONGREGATION

5:19 *Talk among yourselves, using psalms and hymns, and song; and make music to God with all your hearts.*

God's congregation is a fellowship where joy is shared.

The comrades of Francis of Assisi were called God's troubadours. They gave up everything and had but one concern—God's will. God's will was their release from common anxieties. They laughed together. They sang.

We sing. Nothing can suppress our song. Our harp is the heart. As long as it beats, it rhythms a response to the baton of God's love. Genuine, joyful singing is a corporate experience especially rich if it is directed to God, because then it binds us together in him. It also affects the nonsinging hearers. The song of fellowship echoes beyond the fellowship.

We sing psalms. For two thousand years the minds of Christ's followers have been lifted by the magnificent phrases of praise in the psalms. We sing hymns. For two thousand years Christ's followers have written down their faith in God, their confession, their joy, their confidence, and they have sung these hymns together. We sing songs. Perhaps we take current melodies as Charles Wesley did and put to them the message of God's love. Perhaps we take old folk music, as India's villagers do, and use these as vehicles to recite the gospel story.

> Praise the Lord!
> For it is good to sing praises to our God;
> for he is gracious, and a song of praise is seemly.
> (Ps. 147:1 RSV)

There is gladness in song.

"Joyful, joyful, we adore thee, God of glory, Lord of love;
Hearts unfold like flowers before thee, opening to the sun above.
Melt the clouds of sin and sadness; drive the dark of doubt away;
Giver of immortal gladness, fill us with the light of day!"
Amen. [8]

132

THE GRATITUDE OF GOD'S CONGREGATION

5:20 Be thankful to God (who is our Father) always and for everything with the gratitude of our master, Jesus Christ.

God's congregation is a fellowship where thankfulness is shared.

Another characteristic of his fellowship is gratitude. Man's gratitude is his response to God's graciousness. Just as God's graciousness is not requested but given as a natural expression of his love for his creatures, so man's gratitude is not ordered, but given as a natural response of his faith to his creator. Gratitude is not a duty but a spontaneity.

Ten lepers were made well by the compassion of Jesus. One returned to give thanks. He had more than the others, more than health. He had the capacity to show gratitude. His joy at health made him want to share it with him who healed. That is the nature of gratitude. Many have recognized the rich gifts of Providence. Those who return to him with grateful hearts are the people who make up his company.

Those in the company of Christ have the capacity of gratitude for life, for meaning, for joy, for purpose, for kindness, for courage, for people. Their eyes are alert daily to the evidences of goodness, beauty, and truth. They look at every event as an indication of his love. They find his love even in sorrow and suffering, because in these there is hope and victory. Paul and Silas, beaten bloody, stooped in stocks at the Philippi prison, could sing at midnight. So can we if God is with us.

There is greatness in gratitude.

> *"All thy works with joy surround thee,*
> *earth and heaven reflect thy rays,*
> *Stars and angels sing around thee,*
> *center of unbroken praise;*
> *Field and forest, vale and mountain,*
> *flowery meadow, flashing sea,*
> *Chanting bird and flowing fountain,*
> *call us to rejoice in thee." Amen.*[9]

CONSIDERATENESS IN GOD'S CONGREGATION

5:21 *In awe of Christ, subordinate yourselves to one another.*

The congregation of God's people respect one another.

This produces an orderliness absent from the home without disciplining love, and from the social group without a directing faith. Respect is a responsibility for one another absent from get-together crowds, from drinking parties, from beach mobs.

This is a fellowship regulated from within, in contrast to social group manipulation from without. Because of love we prefer one another, subordinate our personal wishes to one another. It is difficult for the world to comprehend such fellowship. "Perish life, but not my stubbornness," said Bhavani in an Indian fable. We would rather die, it seems, than not assert *our* wills. Jesus astonished his friends when he told them, "Whoever would be first among you must be your slave" (Matt. 20:27 RSV). This is not self-effacement, but the confirmation of the importance of the other person to oneself in the fellowship ruled by Christ's spirit.

In our fellowship we support one another. In supporting one another, we support his church (Gal. 6:2).

In all this, Christ is our pattern. In awe of his greatness, his goodness, his enduring love that gathers us, we serve and honor each other.

There is goodness in mutual respect.

"Thou art giving and forgiving,
   ever blessing, ever blest,
Well-spring of the joy of living,
   ocean-depth of happy rest!
Thou our Father, Christ our Brother—
   all who live in love are thine;
Teach us how to love each other,
   lift us to the Joy Divine." Amen.[10]

UNITY IN HOME AND CHURCH

5:22 Wives, live for your own husbands, as you live for God.

Unity in the church has implications for, and is illustrated by, unity in the home.

If we do not have unity in the home, can we have unity in the church? If we have discovered unity in the church, can we learn from this how to have harmony at home? It is based, the letter writer says, on principles of self-giving love and honor. Self-giving love is total loving care for others. Honor is yielding precedence in your life to another and readiness to adapt to another.

Our behavior toward each other is a test for our behavior toward God. A neighbor, for a joke, informed a woman that a great man would be coming to her home for dinner. She prepared a delicious meal. A man came—only her husband. She was disappointed. But was not her husband her great man? And was not she his great woman? Is there not—despite the faults and eccentricities we know so well in each other— is there not something God-given in each of us, even the least of us?

The letter writer asks the wife to adapt herself to her husband. He believed that women show more readiness and more capability to adapt in order to preserve the home; and the home is the key not only to her happiness but to the fellowship of God's people.

One woman said: "God, my husband, and my children come first in my life—in that order. If I do not owe my first allegiance to God, there will be no basis for love in the home. If I do not honor my husband, there will be no base for wholesome security for my children in the home."

She did not mention concern for her privileges. In her self-forgetfulness she demonstrated the all-importance of the woman in the home. Subordinating herself to her calling as wife and mother she becomes the anchor of the home and its uniting force.

God, our Father, may we learn love's respect for one another that thy love may become the atmosphere of our homes. Amen.

LOYALTY IN HOME AND CHURCH

5:23 The husband should be of first importance to the wife, as Christ should be of first importance to the church. It is he who keeps the church alive as his body.

A wife's devotion to her husband keeps the home. The church's devotion to Christ keeps his purpose.

If there are two sides to the question of the husband-wife relationship, this letter takes the woman's side. There is a quip: "A woman accepts a man for the sake of matrimony, and a man accepts matrimony for the sake of a woman." There is a touch of truth in caricature. The truth here is that wives, quite naturally, sense most the importance and security of the home. The letter writer calls on men to love their wives and take responsibility in the home (5:25-29). Here he calls on wives to give their love to their husbands as of first importance in their home lives, as they are to accept Christ as of first importance in their whole lives.

There is no concept in our faith of an arbitrary god to whose inconsistent whims we must submit. God is consistent with his holiness, his justice, and, as we can see in Christ, his love. Subjection of the church to such a God means to carry out the purposes of his holiness, his justice, and his love. In this analogy of man and wife it follows that women are not asked to submit unquestioningly to any arbitrary and irresponsible whim of their husbands or to anything inconsistent with their loyalty to God. But, as the husband is just in his relationships, loyal to Christ, responsible in love to his wife, she is to adapt herself in partnership with his aims and is to support him in every way.

Such a wife is a steadying influence in the home, a star of light for her husband.

God, Father of us all, let us learn from thee the responsibility of love for one another. In our devotion in the home may we find more of thy meaning. And may we take the meaning of devotion into the fellowship of the family of faith. Amen.

CREATIVITY IN HOME AND CHURCH

5:23c, 24 *It is he who keeps the church alive, as his body. But as the church lives for Christ, so should the wife live for her husband in every way.*

As it is Christ who keeps his church alive, it is Christ alone for whom the church must live.

A king took upon himself the protection of his subjects and the promotion of their welfare. His subjects were to subordinate themselves in everything to him. This is the illustration here. Christ, called by the title of kings (Savior or Protector), keeps his church alive. His church serves him.

In the church's subjection to Christ our separate egos are subdued, but not in compliance to a static power. God is not external force. He is an inner compulsion of love. Our very subservience to love creates in us a fierce distaste for anything that violates love. Such rebellion the world does not understand. We love persistently even our enemies while condemning unreservedly the unlove they may practice.

Christ stimulates the church to creative activity in the world. The church is not a finished structure. The church is being built as its people work under Christ's orders. New forms, new practices, will emerge from time to time to express his purpose. But always the church must remain subject to Christ.

Just as the church is entrusted with God's purpose, so are the women of the church entrusted with the homes. She who serves her family in faithfulness to Christ is the happiest of women. She sets an example of orderliness and obedience to her children. Her husband trusts her and relies on her counsel (Prov. 31:26-28).

May Christ rule us, his church. May his spirit live through us that we may be his body, responsive to God's will! O God, our Father, keep us with one another, gentle, wise, and loyal. Amen.

SELF-GIVING LOVE

5:25 Husbands, love your wives the way Christ has loved the church. He gave himself for it.

The beginning of unity is self-giving.

The command is to love. Do we know how to love? Love is the basis of unity in the home. What kind of love is this? Not passion, not mere attraction. Whatever place these may have in conjugal love, they are not the basis for enduring unity. This love, in the context of the company of God's people, is the kind of love with which *God* enables us to love. It is objective, compassionate, whole-souled.

Thus Christ loved the church. Such love is beyond measure. He gave himself for the church. Couriers of an older time handed their messages on to others. Relay racers handed their torches to the next relay men. Christ handed over his very self. He surrendered himself to entrust us with himself—all he has, all he is.

By what Christ did we see what love can be. The church has its being through faith in this kind of love. Because such love is universal, the church is universal when it is the subject of such love. Now we carry his message to the world. We bear his torch.

And we, of the church, are expected to have this kind of love in our homes. The head of the house, among the people of God, is expected to be a man whose love for his wife and family is greater than his love for himself.

This is the beginning of unity. This kind of unity began with Christ and his church. It can be duplicated in our homes. It can unify all people in the family of God.

Give us, God, please, the love that led Christ up to surrender all he had and was for his love of people. Give us his love with which to warm our homes, and with which to light our hearths. Amen.

138

CHRIST'S LIVING LOVE

5:26 Christ gave himself for the church to make it God's people when they had confessed their faith in him—in the act of baptism—and made a clean break with their past.

The completing of unity comes with surrender to him who has given himself for us.

God invites all people to live with the family of God. He invites, and then he comes himself to help us find the way. Like a busy man giving his whole day to help a lost child find his home! He reaches for the child's hand. The child must drop the mudpies from his own before he can take the man's hand. The man takes his grimy hand.

It is like that. We must drop our littleness to accept his greatness. That is the meaning of confession. Confession is offering God all our wrongness in exchange for all his rightness. We exchange our dirtiness for his cleanness. We confess our lostness, and we accept his direction.

There is something about his presence that changes everything for us. Words fail to describe it. So we use similes: clay stains washed off dirty hands, a body bathed. God washes his people clean. His purpose involves making them his people.

Village Balpur in India understood. They had heard about Christ's meaning of God. After many weeks of teaching they were baptized. When the men of Balpur went to the city to work, their fellow workers asked: "What happened to the Balpur men? Their faces are like lights."

Baptism has always been a symbol of this clean break. A break is needed, a surrender to him who surrendered himself for love of us.

Then we become God's people. Unity in the church, unity at home, comes from such love. The possibility of unity among the nations is apparent in such love.

O Father, clean us. We confess our loneliness and the things that have made us lonely, the things we have done and not done that have kept us away from thee. Make us truly thy people. Amen.

RESPLENDENT LOVE

5:27 Christ did this to place the church beside him in splendor, with no spot or flaw, or any other unsightliness. Christ has given the church its special significance and has made it blameless.

The splendor of the church is Christ; the significance of the church is Christ.

The church exists for and by dedication to Christ. Dedication to Christ is not mere bowing down and adoring. Dedication to Christ means standing up alongside him, as it were, in order to do his work with him and to carry on the mission he began. This kind of dedication comes only from the inspiration of Christ himself.

It is this dedication to him in love and service which is the beauty of the church. The bride in her wedding dress, carrying a bouquet, radiant in her joy, is beautiful. So is the church beautiful when it is living its role of the self-forgetful servant. In such a role it truly becomes Christ's.

My home is beautiful with paintings. I did not do them. My father did. The church is beautiful only because of the work of God, the Father. A family in the city is rich because of the fortune their father willed to them. The church's wealth is Christ alone, the gift of God.

A Japanese woman said, "I never felt myself good enough to be Christ's follower. Then I learned that I could come to him as I was and claim his cleanness, associating with others who follow in his company." The church's cleanness is not its own but Christ's.

The building, the organization, the denomination—these are good but expendable frameworks for the church. The people of God re-created from moment to moment in prayer, in repentance, in trust, in partnership with the processes of God's purpose—this is the church. To this church comes God every day to heal and to invigorate.

Heal us from our spots and flaws, O God. Make us Christ's church to stand beside him in battle and in triumph of love. Make thy church beautiful with thee. Make us thy people. Amen.

LOVE CHERISHES

5:28 This is the way husbands should love their own wives —with the same solicitude they have for their own bodies. It could be said that he who loves his wife thereby loves his body.

Christlike love of a man for his wife becomes the basis of his home.

Unlike flaring, subsiding passion, love continues its steady glow. It grows. It gives the wife special significance. The princess-sweetheart of courting days has become a queen for life. Her gentle concern for her husband is her splendor. He centers his attention on the good and pleasant in her through the years. He forgets annoyances or whatever could irritate anything less than love. Her charm is that she is his wife. Her significance is that she is partner of his cares, concerns, pains, and joys.

As Christ must have the partnership of his church to accomplish God's design, so must the husband have his wife's. She is his body, too, and deserves the same solicitude. Her hunger, her need for rest and sleep, for recreation, for health, for meaning are no less important to him than his own. He loves her and cares for her, and she accepts his love. She cares and adapts her life to his. His love is gentle because he cares, strong because it bears responsibility. Yet such love goes beyond responsibility into spontaneous response to the other's need.

Such love is the greatest boon a home can have. Such love is centrifugal. It loves not in order to feed the ego or to find a tense security. It loves in order that each member of the home might grow by love to his or her full expression in society. This is the way Christ loves his church: that each— secure in his love—might serve most fully in his own God-given ways to express God's will in the world.

Now, O God, we pray again for our homes. Expand, with the spirit of Christ, the care we naturally take of ourselves until it grows into love that cherishes one another. O Love of God, fill our hearts. Amen.

LOVE TAKES CARE

5:29-30 For no one is against his own physical well-being. On the contrary, he promotes his health and strength; he takes care of it, just as Christ does his church, which is his body; and we are the limbs of his body.

Unity in the home supports unity in the church.

A home where the head of the house makes it his responsibility to care for his wife and family—such a home can understand Christ's concern for his church. For such love creates a strong bond between the head of the home and the members of the home who become participants in his aims and interests.

Thus, what is called *church* in this letter may not at all be what we have become accustomed to think of as the church. The church, in this letter, is thought of as a unity of relationships in which the people of God are subject to Christ. That is, they participate in his mission. The word used for church once meant an assembly of people summoned together to take responsible action in a mutual affair of the city. The church is a group of people summoned by God to take responsible action in a common cause for "the city of God."

The body is fed and cared for not as an end in itself, but to strengthen it for work. Work to be meaningful must have an aim. The church, the body of Christ, is nourished, cared for, by God's love in order that it have strength to work a meaningful work. We are his limbs. We carry out his aim. His aim is unity.

Wherever God puts us, we can be his limbs, healing, reconciling, unifying. Once we lift eyes to the vision of the unity of man bound in the kindness and goodwill of God, we will find a zest that gives strength to us, who are the limbs of his body. No need, then, to despair. We are parts of his body, and his body is indestructible.

God's people are God's agents of love.

We thank thee, O God, for this privilege of really being alive to eternal meaning and accomplishment. We know thy purpose shall prevail, thy wisdom win. May thy purpose and wisdom direct us as thy church. Amen.

LOVE UNITES

5:31, 32a: *"Therefore, a man shall leave his father and mother*
And shall attach himself to his wife; and the two shall become one."
This is profoundly significant!

Marriage is, by God's design, a basic unit of his purpose for universal harmony.

Unity begins where two in the home become as one. If marriage is only a sex convenience for two separate individuals, it breaks down when passion subsides or fails to synchronize. If marriage is merely the climax of romantic love, it cools in boredom or irritation when the youthfulness, good health, or leisure time of one or both disappear, and the holiday atmosphere is gone.

Real love is the dedication of two people as one to God. Such love endures. It grows. In youth it enables greater sexual compatibility through considerateness. Beyond youth it finds a way to make the honeymoon a lifelong sharing of pleasure, pain, work, and play. It builds the home into the larger, lasting fellowship of all who love God and who ply his love. Such love remains through years.

It is the basic unity—two in the home as one. Glue two sheets of paper together, and they become one sheet, stronger than either of the two before. Tear them apart, and they do not come clean, but torn. No person in a marriage pair is left whole when torn from his mate—except by death, where healing comes with faith and when love holds on.

> Because our inmost beings met and mixed,
> Because thou once hast loved me—wilt thou dare
> Say to thy soul and Who may list beside,
> "Thus she is immortally my bride;
> Chance cannot change my love, nor time impair." [11]

The unity of the home is of profound significance for the church, and so for all society.

Unite, O Father, every husband and wife with thy love. Let them daily turn to thee in prayer. Let thy wisdom teach them patience, thine understanding teach them tenderness. Amen.

LOVE RELATES US

*5:32 This is profoundly significant. But **I** am taking this as a symbol of the relationship between Christ and the church.*

Christ and his church are a profoundly significant relationship.

Who can understand it, however, except they who experience it? It is a shared awareness of those who belong to Christ. Without being able fully to define the wonder of God's meaning, nevertheless we sense the vivid realness of his presence. Christ is the character, the communication, and the warmth of God's presence which our human minds can reach for and apprehend. He is for us no abstract principle, but counsel to our thought, commander of our acts, criterion for our attitudes, consultant for our decisions.

This relationship we have with Christ, however, is ours with him as a church. Our relationship with him is found within his church. As a group we follow him. As a group we balance the life of faith for each other in Christly fellowship.

The relationship of man and wife is used as a symbol of that between Christ and his church. It is a symbol only and is not to be overdrawn. Christ's mission is to connect man with God. And this comes about only as we obey, that is, fall in with his purpose for our lives. The church is responsible to consult the head of the church and to act on his directives.

The symbol of marriage is meaningless for any who do not see in it the responsibility for self-giving, cherishing love on the husband's part and subjection of her self to his life calling on the wife's part. It is not surprising that couples whose relationship to each other is casual, independent, and irresponsible make of church life a relationship with Christ which is casual, independent, and irresponsible.

Yet thou dost love us, Father! Yet thou dost care for us and counsel us. We want to trust thee, heed thee, obey thee so that we may live by thy will for the family, for the church, for the world. Amen.

5:33 Nevertheless, this also applies to you, *as individuals. Every husband among you must love his wife as himself. And let the wife look up to her husband.*

The unity of Christ with his church bears on the relations in the home.

If the people of the church are truly God's people, they serve together in mutual respect and honor—their attitudes clothed in the love of Christ. They will carry these attitudes into the home. God's unity is not outward show. It is inward. It backs the texture of basic human relations.

The love a husband is to show his wife, the letter writer was saying, is affection that carries one's whole personality with it: "Treat your wife with affection as thoroughgoing as your love for your own being." No matter what kind of a body he has, a normal man will take care of it. No matter what kind of a wife he has, a godly man will take care of her. He will not take her for granted. His attentiveness to her will not disappear with years. The letter is not talking about emotional or demonstrative affection, but about steady love.

She looks up to him. A good wife respects her husband as head of the home. She respects his responsibility. She may, indeed, with tactful wisdom, need to build his sense of responsibility, but she does not bypass it. A good wife will commend her husband for his proficiencies and set great store by his abilities. She may, indeed, help him find his abilities. Much of the good which men do for their culture and society has been fortified by the help, advice, and loyal support of their wives.

Unity, however, depends on mutuality—the affection of the husband and the loyal support of the wife! An affectionate husband will loyally support his wife. A loyal wife will give affection to her husband. Yet these are meaningful for unity only when practiced in joint loyalty to the love of God.

Be present, Love of God, at our meals, our rest, our work, and fill the moments in between. Be stronger in our homes than gadgets and dialed entertainment. Love of God, operate through our minds, our hearts, our hands together. Amen.

OBEY YOUR PARENTS

6:1 Children, obey your parents. It is right that you should.

Unity in the church has implications for unity in the family.
Right obedience leads to right freedom.

What is right obedience? It is not the demand for absolute
and unquestioning acceptance of arbitrary orders. The most
arbitrary of parents are the ones for whom God does not exist
as a vital reality. They themselves do not obey God because
they do not understand God. Yet they expect their children to
submit to their whims. Their children are offended by the
lack of solidity and consistency in the parents' demands.
Therefore, the children resort to deceit and trickery in evading
parental rule.

The requirement for obedience in this letter assumes parents
who have a conscious relationship with God. *The root of
obedience is listening.* We are to obey God. But we are to
listen to God and try to understand his will. His orders are
for us to cooperate with his purpose for us. Just so, a child
needs to learn to listen and to cooperate with the purposes of
the home.

Obedience also means prompt response. Harm is done to a
child who is allowed to ignore a request or order from his
parents. By ignoring it a child is testing it—and his parents.
If a parent permits the child to ignore his orders, does he not
show lack of interest in the child? What solid foundation
remains for the child in a home where parents appear to give
little importance to orders given or rules made?

A child learns self-discipline with the help of parents who
set for him responsibilities he is required to carry out day by
day. The older he grows, the more he becomes a consultant
in the making of his rules, but once made they should be
adhered to, unless, by common family consent, they prove to
be unwise. Through wisely led obedience a child grows
toward freedom in self-discipline.

*Father, teach us to obey thy will and to discipline in love the
children thou dost give us. May our homes grow in Christ-
likeness. Amen.*

HONOR YOUR PARENTS

6:2 Honor your father and mother. That is the first rule that contains a promise.

Children's respect for parents, among the people of God, is the beginning of orderly, purposeful society.

For nearly two and a half millennia the Confucianist ideal realized the importance of children's respect for their elders in a stable society. The context of that society, however, was respect for the past. Hence, the stability, while not uncreative, tended, nevertheless, toward stagnancy.

The context of God's people is the forward look toward God's fulfilled purpose. God's purpose gives meaning to a home. The child becomes aware that the parents live for a goal greater than themselves—a goal that influences their behavior and affections. Respect for parents in such an atmosphere gives a child security, links his life to purposive love. Within that love he learns a reverence for life. His own life becomes expressive and meaningful.

Have we loved our children enough to require their respect and obedience? Or have we only indulged them? Indulgence provides no framework for their lives. Do we ourselves hold God in reverence in the home, that children may find at home the basis for orderly society? Do we live with such integrity before them that they can sincerely honor us? Do they perceive our respect for them as persons?

As the child matures, we may encourage him to weigh advice given. A time may come when he will reject advice, but by then he should have learned to establish his reason for rejection of advice, to be frank about it. Subterfuge is neither respect for elders nor respect for self.

He who can honor his parents who honor God builds his life into a framework larger than himself, larger than his home, larger than his universe even—large as God. It is large enough to allow him free movement, but it is, nevertheless, a framework, something to live within and to live by.

Father, we would respect as persons the children among us, for they are thine. In our reverence for thee may we lead our children to honor their parents. Amen.

TOWARD MATURITY

6:3 *The promise is: "that you may prosper and have long life on earth."*

Whoever honors his elders honors himself, for he helps to maintain the kind of ordered society in which he will be able to mature.

Whoever mocks at the dignity of another tramples his own dignity. Thereby he rends the fabric of the society of which he is a part and in which he must find a place. Respect for another, however, is self-respect, for it respects the contribution everyone can make to the social whole. Respect for another is responsibility in society. Disrespect is irresponsibility. Respect is gratitude for what others have done for life. Disrespect is ingratitude. Respect is a step toward maturity. Disrespect is a sign of continued immaturity. Respect is awareness of value in others. Disrespect is blindness to value in others. Respect, therefore, is part of love; it inspires the best in another person. Disrespect, therefore, is part of unlove, for it stirs up the worst in another person. Respect is cheerful; it reflects goodwill. Disrespect is churlish; it reflects ill-will. Respect is constructive in human relations. Disrespect is destructive of human relations. Respect is a response of integrated personalities. Disrespect is a reaction of disintegrated personalities.

He is essentially happy who grows up in a wholesome atmosphere where each person is thoughtful for the welfare of others. He understands others. He feels understood. He expresses a genuine interest in others. The harmony of his emotions makes for a more poised physical being. Medical reports actually state that persons who live in goodwill toward others are more likely to have good health and that their average life-span is longer.

The family among the people of God is a family where respect, love, and good humor are shared.

Father, forgive us that we have ever forgotten to honor thee whom all creation honors. In honoring thee give us the nobility to honor and respect our elders and those who have gone before us. Amen.

GUIDE YOUR CHILDREN

6:4 You, fathers, do not provoke your children to resentment. But educate them in an awareness of God and direct their minds to the meaning of God.

Conscious of God, parents must patiently bring up their children to an awareness of God and his meaning for their lives.

A child needs a father who, in his own consciousness of God as Father, leads his children into a secure awareness of God. A father's own steady relationship with God becomes a guideline for consistency in his relations with his child. Parents who have no guideline, who capriciously cajole or carp at their children, build into them a resentment against all controls. Spasmodic, incoherent overcorrection prods a child to exasperation. Rebellion against parents, unchanneled into personal self-reliance, may be an expression of despair.

Love never relents, never rejects. It provides a sturdy, steady base for children's maturing. Love disciplines; it demands obedience, but to God, not to personal whims. It warns of the immovable justice of God, but in that justice is shown the bedrock of stability on which to build a life.

A parent among the people of God knows that a secular education (education in which God is ignored) for his child is abandonment of his child to uncertainty. It is like putting a child to sea in an anchorless, pilotless boat. The sea is the turbulence of strife and selfishness in the world.

A parent among the people of God knows that the foundation of wisdom is the awareness of God's meaning. Any child educated to this awareness of God tends to be quickened by it in his apprehension of human knowledge. Any normal mind alerted to God's meaning is a challenged mind which responds more readily to the significance of every human experience.

Awareness of God and the meaning of God come best to those children who find them in the consistency of their parents' faith.

O God our Father, ever patient with us, teach us patience with our children. May we walk with them in the direction thou dost lead us. Amen.

149

SERVE YOUR EMPLOYERS WELL

6:5 *Employees, be responsible to your employers—in matters pertaining to your employment—with respectfulness and humility. Do your work with as much sincere dedication as you would give to Christ.*

Unity in the church has implications for unity in employer-employee relations.

The people of God treat their employment as a job to be done honestly, thoroughly, vigorously, as work done for Christ.

When this letter was written, most employees were slaves, completely at their owners' command, with no rights guaranteed, even to life. When this letter is now read, most employees have guaranteed rights and privileges by which they can benefit themselves. Among the people of God the counsel is the same.

The counsel is: "Do your work well. Keep at it. Do not loaf." A free employee has a greater responsibility than a slave. He must understand what he is doing and why. He is responsible to employer, to the users of his services, and to God. He is bound to do his level best and he will—if he belongs to God's people. The counsel is: "Accept your assigned task cheerfully."

Be respectful. Listen readily to the advice of those set over you in your task. Be ready to contribute helpful suggestions. Respect your work. You will grow as your work grows more significant to you.

Be reverent. Christ's followers surrender their personal wishes gladly for the common good. They are not quick to justify or excuse themselves.

Be realistic. Realism to God's people is not the expedient thing but the enduring. That is what makes God's people honest employees, dependable, faithful. They are distinct from counterfeits who pass their hours without diligence and receive their pay without deserving.

Father, the work that we must do this day we would do for thee. Keep us humble. Keep us courteous to all with whom we work. Amen.

WORK WITH A CONSCIENCE

6:6 Do not work merely when under the employer's eyes, or only with an eye to human recognition. Consider yourselves workers for Christ, conscientiously doing God's will.

Link up your work with God's plan.

How can anyone do that? We cannot if we look upon our work as drudgery. We cannot if we see it as a necessary but unpleasant way to stay alive. We cannot if we work well only when we know that we are being watched, or only if we know our advancement and pay depend on it. Also, no matter how well we work, we are far from God's plan if we work simply for recognition or rewards from others.

We can link up with God's plan if we see our work in the light of his purpose. Even a routine assembly-line type of work can be a challenge to cheerful comradeship with fellow workers. We must understand the contribution our own particular job is making, and we can improve on its contribution for wholesome living. If it can make no helpful contribution, we should quit it. We can link up our work with God's plan if it becomes a discipline for our lives, if we work conscientiously, creatively, if we can enjoy a task well done, and make it a reasonable service to God. We can if we work grateful for the work itself, grateful for the people with whom we work, grateful to God. It can if we keep our minds on him.

We can link up with God's plan by making our work a participation in its fulfillment. That plan is for unity—the reconciliation of all God's creatures with him! That plan is only effected by love. Love is the key to workmanship among the people of God. To love our work, to love those who will benefit by it, to love those with whom we work, to love those under whom we work, to love with genuine, spontaneous, unselfish love. This is the way we make evident God's will. This is the way we involve ourselves, with others, in God's plan.

They who work their work for God's will live whole and satisfying lives.

We dedicate our work to thee, O God. We pray for those who will use the product of our labor. We pray for those who direct our work. In whatever we do, thy will be done. Amen.

SERVE GOD'S PURPOSE

6:7-8 *Put your service to good purpose for God, not for men. For you can be sure that each of us, whatever his status in man's social scale, is repaid by God for good workmanship.*

Service, in God's sight, is the hard work we do for the love we bear toward God, toward his purpose, toward his people.

Can you imagine a slave with no privileges, no pleasures, working long and hard and under a whip, but working cheerfully, heartily—bringing a merry spirit to all with whom he serves? The letter writer could. In a time of cruelty to slaves he could imagine God making a man that kind of slave.

The service to which God calls us is no mere religious duty. It is a service possible only in a life overflowing with goodwill. Hearty goodwill and cheerful kindliness should be the mood of every job we do. Because of the love we bear for God's creation we serve him through our work.

This motive drives us to hard work, without looking for luxury and without reaching for reward. It drives us beyond ourselves to work for God. Work for God is work that has enduring meaning. Service to him is serving his love and purpose to other people through our work.

God repays good workmanship for him. Wages to the worker! The reward is not for human goodness. The reward is God's goodness. We are given a chance to work within the goodness of his plan for all men. Whatever our job in the world, whatever our status, we are to work for God and effect his goodness, weave it into the warp of society. The consequences of such work are high wages of joy, satisfaction, and partnership with God.

For *these* wages we have an equal possibility, for we have an equal responsibility to God.

Help us, O God, bring to our work a greater measure of thy love. Cheer us by thy graciousness that we might brighten life for all we meet today. Amen.

RESPECT YOUR WORKERS

6:9 As for you who superintend the work of others, you must show them the same integrity you expect of them. Do not be harsh. For you know very well that both they and you have the same Supreme Employer and he has no favorites.

We have an equal responsibility to each other, and we need to respect each other, for we are equally God's.

The unity God desires among his people straightens out the hierarchy of human society. A vertical society is thrown up by the struggle of self with self within the transiency of time. A horizontal society is laid out by the regard of God's people for all people in the permanency of eternity. Here, power structures are leveled in a way neither aristocrat nor anarchist is willing to recognize.

Here is the letter writer's word to employers, supervisors, managers, executives, foremen, captains, bosses—all the upper men in the power-structure staircases. The word is "behave toward those who serve under you as you would have them behave." You depend for good work on their integrity. They depend on your integrity. You want responsible workers. Be responsible to them. You want their respect. Respect them. You want them to be conscientious. Be conscientious. Should they be loyal? Be loyal to them within your loyalty to God. Should they do their work with goodwill? Show them goodwill—love.

This is the writer's counsel: be neither boastful nor threatening. Harshness in language, in attitude, in directives may make people hustle, but this is the hustle of disunity. It shreds the fabric of social cohesion. For people who feel threatened, work becomes their despair, not their pride.

In God's sight we are equally employees under his rule. Bound to him we are brothers.

Master, God, great employer of our lives, point out to us our tasks. Inspire our work together, in respect for one another's minds, for one another's handiwork, and for one another's needs. Amen.

BE STRONG

6:10 *From now on, all of you, be powered by God, vigorous in the vitality that comes from him.*

Together, in unity with God, is the strength of life's meaning.

From now on let the course of our lives be in the stream of his love. Cut a channel from the pond to the stream, and its water, mingling with many waters, is drawn by the pull of gravity to the sea. Cut a channel from our lives to the stream of God's activity, and the energies of our lives, mingling with the energies of many lives, are drawn by the pull of God's purpose toward fulfillment.

A still and stagnant, turbid water joined to a moving stream becomes a splashing, sparkling torrent piling up power as it moves toward the ocean. Our lives, mentally muddled and confused, when joined to the stream of God's people become meaningful, clear, forceful, expanding energy.

The stream's power is gathered from gravitation that pulls it down to the sea. Our strength is gathered from him who rules our destiny. Dissipation of human energies is due to lack of awareness of God's rule or of his presence. He is our strength (I Tim. 1:12). His is our might. Strength flows through us as we reach toward him (Rom. 4:20). The dynamics of God pulsates through us when we rise above our muddy banks to join his flood of love.

Obviously, then, our strength is more than ours. God draws from us all our energies so that we have none left to expend upon ourselves. His task demands all the potentialities of his church, multiplied by his power. God's will led Christ to Gethsemane (abandonment of self-will for God's). It led him to Calvary (expression of God's will for man). It leads us, too. It led Jesus to places of greatest need, sorrow, sin. It leads us, too. His strength means action that releases renewing power in the earth.

God, we are weak! Yet we rise to the strength thou dost inspire. Help us from our weakness to live vigorously by thy vitality. Amen.

READY FOR BATTLE

6:11 *Get into the battle equipment God gives you so that you may be able to stand up to the stratagems of his adversary.*

God enables us to outface disintegrating influences.

Yet the stratagems of God's antagonist are great. God's antagonist is whatever would disintegrate our lives from his integrative meaning, thus pulling us to pieces; whatever seeks to contradict the purpose God provides us, thus creating confusion; whatever seeks to overturn the values his love lends us, thus shattering standards; whatever seeks to undermine the stability faith in him forms for us, thus leaving us to teeter on a tightrope of guesses over a gorge of deep uncertainties.

God's antagonist beats the drum of prejudice and fear but laughs derision at love and hope. It cheers at bombast, jeers at sympathy. The stratagem of God's antagonist is to ridicule faith and ostracize believers, to misinterpret virtues of courage and courtesy and to champion the vices of self-indulgence until the coward feels his gun and his bottle are marks of bravery, his recklessness and callousness signs of virility. God's antagonist jazzes up the moment and leaves the hour of life tuneless. It fizzes up the glass tonight and leaves the plate empty on tomorrow's table.

The church is called to unabashed combat against God's antagonist. God gives us combat equipment. God arms us for battle, defense and offense. We are champions for the meaning of God against all that is God-lacking in ourselves and in our world. God's people should be known by their battle dress, by their uniform goodwill, by God's time-over-ruling will.

We are to make our stand with God, stand firm, stand fast. We are to endure with him who endures with us through thick and thin. Our unity with him and with his people makes it possible for us to stand. No house divided against itself can stand.

Equip us, God, to battle bravely and wisely against life's adversary. Unite us together in thy strength. Amen.

THREATS TO PERSONHOOD

6:12 Our struggle is not against human enemies. It is against dehumanizing threats to our personhood.

Ours is a strugggle of the mind for ultimate meaning and of the heart for enduring relationships.

The conflicts that rack the world in overt war, riot, raging accusations, and in covert bitterness are symptoms. They symptomize deep inner conflicts of societies caught in cultural vacuums and of individuals trapped in emptiness. Like a beaten boxer, society swings at the blows of unseen forces, individuals sway at the punch of demonic pressures.

The people of God are people in the world, and so we, too, face these forces and pressures.

What is our struggle? Said a college student: "The trouble is that we can't even struggle. How can we fight empty space? All we seem to have out there is one big lack of anything real." "Darkness" the letter writer described it. "Emptiness" the college student called it. "Without God life has no destiny," the letter writer wrote. "It has no meaning," the student said.

"We live in a dehumanizing world," one woman said. "In such a world how can I relate to God or to any person? Life is all in little pieces that do not seem to fit." Without God's vital force in life there is a power failure of positive cohesiveness.

In such a world ancient man felt surrounded by malicious superhuman forces. In such a world modern man feels threatened by anxieties and guilts. The oneness of his being, his wholeness as a person, is slowly shattered. Ancient man was a plaything in a universe of gods and demons, of helpful and harmful elements. Modern man is tossed about in a void of irrelevant yearnings, in an abyss of fears.

O God, be with our minds as we struggle in thought, with our spirits as we struggle for self-control, with our hearts as we struggle with affections and loyalties. O help us. Amen.

WHAT RULES YOU?

6:12 *Our struggle is . . . against threats to our personhood, against standardization.*

Ours is the struggle of the mind for ultimate meaning and of the heart for enduring relationships.

What rules our lives? Inner appetites? Outer pressures? Goals we have set ourselves? Or goallessness? The unrelated ego is the most cruel, arbitrary, and illogical of tyrants. Other rulers that demand our allegiance are political movements and religious dogmas. This age of science has spawned an amazing number of sophisticated superstitions. Many submit to the rule of the organization in which they work. To conform to its pattern is their religion. And for many there is a shadow-ruler—the present material moment invests our interests and time and defies the rule of eternal Spirit.

What is the authority in our lives? By what do we measure value? By the organization—political, religious, social, or professional? Do its expediences decide our day-to-day ethics? Are we in the "church," and yet adapt our principles to the code of our jobs? Do we go along with the team with which we work in methods contrary to the spirit of Christ? Do we put confidence in standards that are false if God is truth? These are times of standardization. Do we make standards in society that disregard those of the church, as though the church were irrelevant?

For many there is no authority but that which they may find from day to day, from newspaper to newspaper, from TV ad to TV ad. Secularism robs him who trusts its authority of personal integrity and identity. A frightened civilization can choose a variety of social ideologies which provide insolent authority. Many choose them who, without confidence in God, have lost their understanding of themselves as persons. They are willing to become cogs in a depersonalized political machine, because cogs, at least, have a place.

O God, Creator, be our ruler, lest we be ruled by fear. Let Christ be the authority in our lives, lest we be moved by anything less than love. We accept thy rule. We cling to thine authority. Amen.

PRESSURES

6:12 Our struggle is . . . against the pressures of feverish activity in a universe that seems empty of sense, a struggle for ultimate meaning against forces of futility.

Ours is a struggle of the mind for ultimate meaning and of the heart for enduring relationships.

What pressures our lives? The letter writer's contemporaries felt that they were surrounded by unseen, cosmic powers of the world of darkness. So do our contemporaries, although the figures are changed. We have new names for psychological and social pressures, but our fears are just as real, and so are our uncertainties. In rapid social change, in broken human relations, men dread the intangible difficulties which they seem powerless to master or escape. Under the constant menace of total and instant annihilation by bombs the future seems futile.

We whirl in feverish activities, and we do not know why. We strive to express ourselves in new ways, but we do not know for what. We who consider ourselves free are victims of a cluster of demands. We who consider ourselves educated are bombarded with a mass of information and knowledge without meaning. We who have leisure to be entertained are satiated with violence without values, sex without secrets. We feel ourselves to be but pawns of power struggles, digits in the masses, submerged to uselessness.

In our reaction to the pressures in and about us, are we losing our ability to respond to God's plan?

There is struggle in life, and no escape from it. But there is meaning. Meaning unfolds itself to him who struggles for it. Ours is the struggle for meaning against meaninglessness, for right answers against false answers. We struggle toward him who is the answer, and false answers no longer disturb. We join him who is meaning, and meaninglessness no longer distorts.

Father, because we are thine but are at the same time part of the world's human struggle, help us. Help us in our struggle to find thy design in the midst of man's disorder. Amen.

STAND UP TO DISTRESS

6:13 This is the reason you need to get into the battle dress God provides you. Then you will be able to keep your balance in time of crisis and, having subdued all adversity, to keep your stability.

In an unsteady world of change and anxiety we need to be sure with God's assurance.

God does not give us a hideaway. He gives us equipment for combat. He calls, "Come." We come and he says, "Go." But first he equips us for our going. We are God's people when we come to worship him. We are God's people when we go to battle for him. For worship is a time to be equipped by God to live in the world. So in time of crisis we need not be resigned to helplessness. We are equipped to meet crisis head on.

But you must drop whatever self-interest you have been carrying if you are to take his equipment. The soldier going into battle is not the soldier going on leave. "Take on the whole armor of God," wrote the ancient letter writer: "shield, helmet, breastplate, greaves, sword, lance" for offensive warfare. Be ready for battle, people of God. Pain and perplexity, problems and pressures will challenge your best, but God's spirit will cheer you on. You know you can be more than conquerors with the aid of him who loves you (Rom. 8:37).

Goodness for life you gain by your labor. Meaning for life you discover by your effort. Victory in life you win by your struggle. But God is the goodness and the meaning and the victory. And God gives us the tools for our labor, the map for our discovery, the combat equipment for our victory.

For always remember, you do not struggle alone. We struggle together—we of the church. The battle dress is fitted to the body of Christ which is the church. We steady each other. We stand together. We keep our balance when the world rocks. When shocks come we still stand. We keep standing. Our stance is Christ.

Father, we come to thee to be commissioned by thee. Arm us with minds and spirits equal to the difficulties we face, and more than equal, for the sake of others who may need our help in their struggles. Amen.

HOLD YOUR GROUND

6:14 *So stand your ground, with firm conviction, prepared to strike, wearing integrity like a bulletproof vest.*

Our defense is integrity in action. Our offense is integrity in the expression of our faith.

The emphasis of this passage in the letter is personal genuineness. The call is imperative. Face every crisis, every problem, with sure faith, unmixed with self-interest, unshadowed by self-deception. Plunge into life with sure love, unmasked, clear-motived, clean-minded, and you are proof against the bullets of despair, of disturbed emotions that whirl around an axis of fear.

Truth is like a belt around the body of God's church. It permits the church to be free-moving, quick, assured, bold in action. Truth is the knowledge we possess and which possesses us. It is our firm conviction of him who is the truth. Truth is the consequence of courageous search for him who has captured us, for he is God of truth. Truth is what we have seen in Christ. Truth is our experience of God's realness in life, and our practice of God's meaning in life—in daily work, in politics, in economics, in religion. Truth is opposite to sham. It is deeper than appearance. It affects our words with sincerity, our works with honesty, our attitudes with frankness, our self-evaluation with candor. Truth confronts the power interests, the counselors of expediency, the scientists in laboratories—confronts them with their responsibilities in man-to-man relationships.

Right living, right doing, right thinking straps a bulletproof vest around the body of God's people. Protected by integrity in all our dealings we can champion integrity before the world. Integrity means we have no secrets, fears, pride, or self-righteousness dividing us. It means we are well-balanced, sane in our view of life and in our attitudes—if we have integrity. It means to trust each day to God.

Father, make us ready to face anything with thee. Keep us true in action, true in witness, true to thee, to ourselves, to each other. Amen.

NEWS OF PEACE

6:15 Have your communications system in readiness to send out the good news of peace.

God's church must be made of steady people, at all times and in any situation ready to give clear expression to the good news of peace, to the assurance that God is in control.

Peace is God's harmony, the concord of life fitted to God's purpose. Peace is God's wholeness, the health of a mind conscious of God's presence. Peace is God's design, the order of a society conformed to God's plan. Peace is God's unity, the centering of a people confident in God's person, Christ. Peace is God's might, the energy of a faith controlled by God's power.

God's peace is ours to transmit to the world:

> How beautiful upon the mountains
>   are the feet of him who brings good tidings,
> who publishes peace, who brings good tidings of good,
>   who publishes salvation,
>   who says to Zion, "Your God reigns." (Isa. 52:7 RSV)

Messengers, foot-runners in ancient times, brought good news of peace and victory. Such runners wore sturdy shoes, well thonged so as not to come off. Today the emphasis would be, perhaps, not on shoes but on electronics. To the waiting people on Mt. Zion, worried about the battle, the runner's cry was cheering. "Peace! Peace! Victory! God still reigns!" For a world waiting for God and yet not knowing him, for a world wanting a fixed point of certainty and yet confused, this assured announcement will be good news: "Peace! Peace! Your God does reign! God is still in charge! God *is!*"

> *"Drop thy still dews of quietness,*
> *till all our strivings cease;*
> *Take from our souls the strain and stress,*
> *and let our ordered lives confess*
> *the beauty of thy peace." Amen.*[1]

161

COMMITMENT TO TRUST

6:16 Especially take up the shield of commitment to God. With this you will be able to put out all the flaming missiles of your enemy.

Commitment to God quenches the destructive influences that vex a life.

Commitment to God does not avoid trouble. It sometimes makes us the focus of antagonism in a troubled world. The farther the church advances into the heart of society to carry through God's purpose, the more will its enemies attack the church. The higher we rise to the heights of integrity with God, the stronger seem the threats.

The destructive influences in our lives are those that distract us from God's design for us. "Anything which opposes this evolution in the moral and spiritual realm, anything which tends . . . to replace man under the dictature of the body is contrary to the directing Will and represents absolute Evil." [2]

We can close the door against all influences that would divide us from God's will for us. There is a shield impenetrable as rock. The shield is trust. The shield is life entrusted to God. Thereby we become trustworthy. If we commit our lives to him, his purpose dominates. Commitment leads us to live consistently by what we believe. We bank on God and find his credit sound.

Commitment to God commits us to trust in one another. We trust each other's faith. We do not try to make each other like ourselves, or parrots of our creeds. Our common trust in God, the common path we walk following where Christ has walked is cause enough for trust in one another. In that trust we cannot be burned by the missiles of suspicion, of insincerity, of separateness from one another and so from God.

O God, we commit ourselves to thee. Joined to one another we would be faithful to thy will, that by thy will we may not fall under any influence that would separate us from our unity in loyalty to Jesus Christ, our Master. Amen.

SHIELDED

6:16 *Especially take up the shield of commitment to God. With this you will be able to put out all the flaming missiles of the enemy.*

Faith is our shield. Faith is confidence in God. Faith is loyalty to God.

A man without faith is foolhardy. He makes no more sense than a sailor who would prefer a raft at sea to the duties of shipboard life. The sea might be calm when such a sailor makes his choice, the air balmy; the carefree life of a raftsman might seem pleasant. Until the storm comes! A man without faith makes no more sense than a soldier who would prefer a stroll in no-man's-land to the discipline of army life in war. The front might be quiet when such a soldier makes his choice, the jungle chattering with wild life, beautiful with color; the carefree life of a wanderer might seem pleasant. Until the firing starts!

The man in mental anguish with no reference for his life knows how fiery that anguish is. The woman with a heartache and no certainty to cling to knows how flame-filled her ache can be. The youth mixed up, without a pointer to steer by, knows how thick the missiles fly. People in distress run madly to any shelter, fall into any foxhole. So cults and demagogueries thrive where frightened people live.

But there is always God. He cares. He also commands. We come to him, and his love controls us (II Cor. 5:14). His wisdom stimulates our intellects. His care calms our emotions. His final cause directs our lives. Then we desire his discipline. We delight in duty done for him.

We are confident in him. This is our shield. Nothing can daunt us now. We remain loyal to him. This is our protection. We disdain attachment to any pattern less true than he. We spurn as fantasy any idea or program for life less real than he.

Lord God, transcending space and deep within our minds thou art. Longer than time and still within each moment thou art. Greater than thy universe yet to us a Father thou art. We dedicate ourselves to live in confidence by thee. Amen.

163

ATTACK

6:17 *And put on the helmet he gives you (he who makes your life secure with him). And take the weapon his spirit gives you—God's orders.*

Trust God! Follow his orders! Attack!

The church is meant to be God's army, attacking everything that scatters and fetters people, that divides them and destroys their personeity. The church is meant to restore them to their God. The church cannot do what it is meant to do unless it follows God's orders.

Our "helmet" is the security he gives us. It is the restoration of our minds and of our attitudes to God. The Christlike mind and Christlike attitudes become crash helmets that protect our sanity and sense in any circumstance that jars society. We do not go out of our minds when crises shatter the normal existence we knew, because God—whom we understand in Christ—has been our well-being, and he will be the consummation of all to which we look forward. As Jesus walked steady in his time, so can we in ours.

We do not remain detached, however, from the world and its crises. Trust in God thrusts us into tensions. Our weapon, unlike a gun, is no destructive instrument of human cowardice. It is the constructive instrument of divine concern. It is the weapon God's spirit gives us. Unlike a bayonet that tears the flesh, God's spirit heals. The church that trusts in God is entrusted with his spirit to enter the thick of society and heal its wounded.

God's spirit is his spoken order. His spirit is his word of command to his commandos. Attack with his love's wisdom and with his wisdom's love! People of God, unite to attack man's disunity! Attack to unite them to God's plan!

The secure life is life lived actively and eagerly at God's orders.

We would put on the protective helmet of trust in thee, our Father, God, that we may be saved from ourselves and for thyself. Give us thine orders. Use us at thy will. Amen.

164

IN TOUCH WITH GOD

6:18 Be continually in prayer, referring everything to God. Keep your mind on him all the time. Be alert about it. Persist in it, and be in prayer for all God's people.

Stand firm! As God's people we must continue to apply ourselves to God, to apply God's wisdom to ourselves, to apply God's love to others.

God's purpose is an ongoing thing. Our commitment to it is a daily thing. Constantly we are to direct our minds to God. Continually we are to take council with him. Prayer maintains our communion with God. Without prayer God becomes a stranger to us.

God's provision meets our needs. We do not pray for things we selfishly would like. We pray only for direction in our lives lived for him. Prayer maintains perspective on ourselves. Without prayer we become strangers to ourselves.

God's providence is for everyone. We surround others with God's concern. Prayer maintains our fellowship with others. We cannot hold grudges against nor be indifferent to those for whom we pray with goodwill.

Prayer is our exercise of faith. The prayerless rush of activities done in God's name makes us flabby, makes the church feeble. Prayer strengthens us. It is a habit of mind. It is an attitude of love.

Prayer is God's spirit leading us. It is not our groping. It is his guiding. It is not crying in the dark. It is listening in the light.

Prayer is alertness to God and, at the same time, to the world around us. It is looking at the present from the vantage of God's future. It is day-by-day aliveness to God's will (Rom. 12:11).

Prayer is persistent adherence to God.

Our Father, lift us from the squalor of our selfishness. Raise us from the poverty of our petty wishes. Let thy presence be known to us and to all thy people. And through us all thy will be done. Amen.

6:19 *And pray for me that the right words may come to my mind when I open my mouth to speak, that I may boldly, freely, and clearly communicate the meaning of God's purpose.*

We must, with God's help, try to make people understand the meaning and intent of life.

There were secret religions in those days. None but the initiates understood them. He risked his life who revealed their secrets to noninitiates. The letter writer, having been let in on the secret of God's plan, wants to tell everyone. The secret is that God has a plan for everyone. He would draw all his creatures together in a great community of love and fellowship, with all barriers down, all fears banished. The community of Christ's followers are in on the secret. How can they keep the secret if they really believe it, since it is for everyone?

The church exists to spread the secret widely and boldly. We become a part of God's universal unity by participating in the business of making it universal. To communicate this knowledge the church must speak to peoples' understanding, help them give attention to what they have always heard but did not heed. The letter writer asked for prayer, and every spokesman of this message needs the prayerful support of God's people. (Prayer is an order to witness to what we know.)

But where are the people of God? Who are they? Do they witness to what they know? Do they even know? Are they, indeed, God's people? A religion has grown up with worn-out words that hide God's message and lock up Christ's meaning. Traditions few understand encrust the most dynamic news the world could ever hear. We are even casual about it. Let us get the message through. Let us understand it, understand its relevance to life, and then speak boldly, freely, clearly.

God's purpose! His universe is shot through and through with the great sweeping, living love. This love completes a life and gives it power over existence.

Great God, Father of us all, we do not ask for ease or comfort but for the ability to communicate thy purpose to our fellow men. So teach us to tell them the meaning and intent of life. Amen.

IN TOUCH WITH HEARERS

6:20 (For this I am an ambassador—in custody.) Pray that when I tell it, I may speak freely as it is necessary for me to speak.

Whatever our condition, we are witnesses to what we live by or to what we fail to live by.

He may have been an old man, he may have been in prison —the man who wrote this letter. Yet he spoke with the confidence of an ambassador of God! He announced the good news of God's peace, of God's provision for humanity. Some heard it jubilantly. Others did not understand. Instead of a welcome or the diplomatic immunity of an "ambassador," they jailed him. But even in jail he could not keep quiet. His message of God's universal love was also for those who jailed him. His problem was to make them understand.

Our problem is to make the people understand. When we speak in archaic terms, in unworldly language, or when we muffle the news we bring in ritual religious terms, we stop their ears. When "nationalist" groups become intolerant of ideas that challenge them, and when ideological groups try to suppress any universal faith, they stop their own ears.

Nevertheless, we cannot keep silent about it. An African imprisoned for his message wrote to a friend: "We speak daily of the expectation we have in Christ. Hundreds have already heard and accepted Christ's leadership for their lives." An Asian imprisoned for publicly declaring his faith said to a friend, "Don't try to free me. I have found here an eagerness of those who come and go to hear the good news."

When we speak plainly in words our hearers understand, they respond to our explanation of God's rule over today and his purpose for tomorrow. When they see our lives dominated by the goodwill of God's spirit, they respond. At such times may we speak the right word they need to hear, that they may join us among God's people—reconciled.

> *"O teach me, Lord, that I may teach*
> *the precious things thou dost impart;*
> *And wing my words, that they may reach*
> *the hidden depths of many a heart." Amen.*[3]

WE KEEP IN TOUCH WITH EACH OTHER

6:21 I am sending this letter with Tychicus. He is one of us in God's family—a dependable worker, loyal to the Master. Because you also are interested in knowing how things are with me, he will tell you everything I am doing.

We keep in touch with each other.

The unity of God's people is maintained through their contact with each other across geographical distances and human differences. Our fellowship is open.

Paul kept in touch. His life was open—an open book of adventure for God. He hid nothing. What he experienced, what he learned of God in his experience, what he did, were of interest to his fellow followers of Christ. He had affection for them. He wrote them letters. He sent friends like Tychicus to report to them and to bring news of them back to him (Col. 4:7-10). This became a practice in the church—to report, to share experiences, to learn from one another, to extend around the world a fellowship of prayer and love.

We keep in touch. Our fellowship is open. We hide nothing. We have no barriers among us if Christ is our Master. In God's love we are one. Indifference to one another would be irresponsibility to God.

We commune with God and communicate with each other. We need to write to one another as groups, send friends to one another, to listen to one another, to learn from one another —to extend our fellowship. We must share our understanding of God's meaning. We must give and accept counsel from one another, give and accept assistance. God's purpose is not divided, nor can we be divided if we are his.

People such as Tychicus are threads that weave the fabric together. They carry God's message wherever they go. When they meet together it is not as delegates of local congregations or as their representatives. They meet as God's delegates, his representatives to one another.

Our Father, in whom we have our unity, in the spirit of love may we receive one another and keep our fellowship intact. Amen.

WE COMMUNICATE COMMUNITY

6:22 That is why I am sending him to you—to let you know all about us and to draw us closer together.

The people of God are to communicate with one another and to maintain community.

Early followers of Christ thought of themselves as the people of God's coming day. In the scattered companies of God's people the brother of one is brother to all. So Tychicus was accepted wherever he went. He was sent not merely to report on Paul's group and advise with the groups he visited. He was also sent from congregation to congregation to renew and inspire their loyalty to each other and to their one God. Like Tychicus, we are all chosen, we are all commissioned to renew and inspire God's community among us.

We, as God's people, meet together or send visitors from our congregations to meet together. We do this to discuss our common hope and faith and concerns. We come together as many congregations in one town, or in area, regional, or world-wide consultations to inform one another about what we are doing. We draw together in counsel, courage, comradeship. God's mission of reconciliation to the world is effected only through our reconciliation with one another. Our fellowship leaps across man-made barriers. It demonstrates the community of love to which all men are invited.

We thank thee, O God, our Father, for the members of thy family around the world. We thank thee for their commitment to thee and for the inspiration they bring to us. Amen.

PEACE AMONG US

6:23 *Best wishes to you, my brothers; may peace be yours and may you have the love with integrity that comes from God our Father, and from the master, Jesus Christ.*

When we are with the Father, then we have peace with our brothers.

This letter began with greetings to God's consecrated people. God's people look to him as to a Father. On the basis of this relationship they are brothers. God's love binds them to him and to one another. They bear a family resemblance. That resemblance is their confidence in God and their loyalty to Jesus Christ.

The letter closes with a wish for peace. Peace is the health of the body of God's people, the welfare of his family. Peace is our relationship of goodwill. It grows from love, God's love.

Peace grows from confidence. Our faith in God is given us by God. We did not say, "I will imagine something nice and good and believe in it as God." God who created us gave us faith—and met us in our needs and yearnings. As we trusted him our confidence in him grew. We grew more confident in ourselves as his people, instruments of his will. We grew more confident in each other.

Peace is not yet absence of turmoil, but the presence of God, the Father, in the middle of turmoil. If we are unconscious of God we get sick in turmoil, distressed. Conscious of his presence, we keep steady for he is steady. God with us, we can have joy even in turbulence.

Peace is not the lack of tension but the mastery of it in loyalty to Jesus Christ. When God's spirit controls our lives, tension can be tuned to his pitch, played to his praise, harmonized to his theme.

The marks of the people of God are peace and love and faith in brotherhood. We are the people who live in great expectation.

Our Father, give us peace to live in the brotherhood of thy family. Give us love to love the world together—with thy love. Give us faith to live by mutual trust in thee. Unite us in loyalty to one master, Jesus Christ. Amen.

LOVE FOR EVER

6:24 May the graciousness of God's love be among all of you who love our master, Jesus Christ. For Ever.

Now we know what "grace" is—the gracious presence of God's love that unites us.

Grace cannot be understood apart from reconciliation, nor reconciliation apart from God. God made us. God called us to be his people. God came to us and made it possible for us to know him. It is in knowing God we come to know what we are and what we are meant for. That is how we come to know each other. We are meant to belong to God, to his people, to one another.

We know this because God has made it clear to us by Jesus Christ. In him, as man, we see what God can be like. His followers were joined together from many walks of life by their love for him. They understood the magnitude of his love, of God's love, when the cross took him from their fellowship: they discovered that the love remained. Nothing could kill their love for him. It lived. Because it lived, their fellowship lived—it could not be broken up.

The fellowship grew strong from nation to nation around the world, from generation to generation. We belong to that same fellowship of Jesus Christ. Nothing can separate us if we belong to him. We love him with an inextinguishable love, for he is for us the meaning of God.

We love him with the indestructible love he gave to us, the love God gives to us. That love is the grace that permeates our brotherhood. We are his. So we are one another's. This is his plan. This will be the fulfillment of his plan as we extend his love to all creation—and through all the generations.

For Ever.

O God, our Father, may the grace of thy love be in thy church. May nothing ever quench our love and loyalty to Jesus Christ. Complete through us thy purpose of unity for all creation. Amen.

THE EPHESIAN
LETTER

1:1 From—Paul, special messenger of Christ Jesus, sent out by God's will.

To—God's consecrated people who keep faith with him in loyalty to Christ Jesus.

1:2 Grace and peace be yours from God our Father and our master Jesus Christ.

1:3-6 So very good is God, the Father of our master, Jesus Christ, who has done such good things for us through Christ in all that goodness which is vital because it relates us to the eternally best. For, as a matter of fact, before the beginning of the universe he chose us to become, in union with Christ, his own recognized and guilt-free children living in his presence in love. He had already designed for us the relationship with him of children through Jesus Christ. This was in line with the goodwill of his purpose—thanks to the reality of his gracious deed with which he has graced our lives, through him in whom he delights!

1:7-14 In him we are released by means of his self-given life—we are forgiven for having failed to live as God intended. This is all in line with the rich goodness of his gracious care which he has lavished upon us. He has even made it possible for us to have awareness and discernment (which we did not have before) into his purpose. This is in line with his plan which he had already arranged in Christ. His plan to bring about the fulfillment of history is to unite under Christ every-thing in the universe. Belonging to Christ, we also have our definite assignment in this plan of his by which he operates everything in line with his resolved purpose—that we, when we had placed our confidence in Christ, should be evidence of his reality. Belonging to Christ, when you had heard the message of truth, the good news of your liberation, and be-longing to Christ, when you had placed your trust in him, *you* also were identified by his promised spirit, his very pres-ence. His spirit is the first part of our inheritance to come—a receipt for that which is saved up for us, as evidence of his reality.

1:15-23 Because of this, and because I heard of the faith among you who are under the influence of the master, Jesus, and of your love for all who are consecrated to God, I never cease to be thankful for you, and to be thinking of you in my prayers that the God of our master, Jesus Christ, the gloriously real Father, may give you a wise and discerning spirit that you may come to know him better, that the eyes of your inner mind be illumined to see clearly what is the great expectation to which he calls you and what is the wealth of reality which falls to you in the heritage he provides his people, and how immeasurably vast is his power for those of us who place their confidence in him. This power is as great as the energy of his conquering strength which he put to work in Christ when he had raised him from the dead and had placed him in the most significant position: along with him who rules all that is of eternal meaning far above any rule and authority and power and dictatorship and above any person that could be called on—not only in these times, but in times to come. God has arranged everything under Christ—he has placed everything under his feet, and he has made him head over everything and he gave him to the church. The church is his body, the completion of him who completes God's meaning in every way.

2:1-10 And you, you were dead in your wrongdoing and in your misdeeds which you were in the habit of doing, following the customs of the times, following the lead of the ephemeral ideas of your surroundings, the spirit which at the present

173

time operates among those who have nothing in which to trust. In their company we all once passed our time—yielding to physical desires, carrying out the inclination of human passion and notions; like the rest of them we were just naturally creatures of impulse. But God, rich in compassion because of the great love with which he loved us who were dead in our wrongdoing, has made us alive together with Christ (for remember: it is by his gracious power you are restored). And he raised us together with Christ and also gave us together with Christ a place supreme with him so that he might clearly show to the succeeding ages the immeasurable resources of his gracious kindness to us through Christ Jesus. For it is by the power he graciously uses in your behalf that you are restored when you rely on him. This is not your own doing. It is the gift of God. It did not result from your efforts. You've done nothing to boast about. God made us what we are: created, in relationship with Christ Jesus, to carry out the good work for which he has provided. Doing his good work is to be the conduct of our lives.

2:11-19 Therefore, remember that at one time, due merely to the fact of your physical birth among another people, you were considered outsiders by those who, due merely to the act of a religious rite, considered themselves insiders. Far from sharing their expectation of the Messiah, you were excluded from the community of Israel. You were strangers to the agreement which carries for them the promise of God's purpose—without a great hope to look forward to, without God in the world. But *now,* associated with the Messiah Jesus, *you* who used to be remote from us have become close to us. We are centered together by Christ's act—his self-given life for us. For it is he who brings us together, he who made our two groups one, who broke the barriers down that separated us, which had made us hostile to one another. He, by the very nature of his life on earth, did away with an order of relationships based on rules and regulations so that he might create, through our personal relatedness to himself, a united new humanity. This is the way he brings about peace. He did this by way of the cross that he might reconcile both groups as one body, joined to God, having brought our hostility to an end in himself. For when he came among us he brought the glad message of peace to those of you who were far off and peace to those who were near by. Because it is through him that we, both from far off and from near by, united in the same spirit, have access to the presence of the Father. Now, therefore, no longer are you foreigners and strangers away from home, but you are fellow citizens with God's consecrated people, family members at home with God.

2:20-22 This house is built on foundations laid with those who have been God's spokesmen and with those who have been his envoys. The corner foundation stone is Christ Jesus himself. About this corner foundation stone the entire structure is fitted and grows into a sanctuary sacred in its relationship to the Master. Joined to him, you also are built into the structure along with others as a place for God to inhabit.

3:1-13 This is the reason that I, Paul, am a prisoner of Christ Jesus in your behalf—you people of the nations. You must have heard of my commission to bring to you an awareness of the love, power, and wisdom God has for you. I have already written to you briefly about the disclosure by which the hidden meaning was explained to me. By reading what I have written, you will understand my insight into the deeper meaning of Christ—which was not made known to people of other generations as it is now disclosed by his spirit to his own messengers and spokesmen who are consecrated to him— that the people of the nations might inherit with us, and share with us, as one people, and participate with us in the promise proclaimed through Christ Jesus. I have become a servant of this good news. For this task God's gracious gift is given to me, his strength is at work in me. Even to me, less than the least of all God's people—to me was given this privilege joyfully to proclaim to the people of the nations the untrackable riches of the Messiah. God, who created all things, has always had a secret purpose for his creatures. It has always been obscure to men, however, through their lack of comprehension of the meaning of God. To make God's arrangement clear to all men: this is my privilege. That through the church the infinitely varied wisdom of God might now be made known to those in places of highest rule and authority—in line with the design of the ages which he put into effect through Christ Jesus our master! Joined to him, we are reassured in him, and thus come to God with confidence, trusting in him. So I ask you not to be discouraged by my troubles for you—by which God becomes real to you.

3:14-19 This is the reason I fall on my knees before the Father from whom his whole family—gathered to him and scattered in the world—has its identity. May God give you from his rich realness the capacity for inward strength enabled by his spirit. As you rely on him, may Christ live in your hearts. May your lives be rooted and grounded in love so that you might be strong enough to grasp for yourselves—in company with all God's consecrated people—what the breadth, the length, the height, the depth of Christ's love may be, so that you might know the love of Christ, which is more than all knowledge; so that you might be mature in the maturity which is of God!

3:20-21 Now to him who by the exertion of his power among us can do far more than we would ask or conceive: to him may his splendor (seen in the church and in Christ Jesus) direct attention through all the generations and through all time. May it truly be so!

4:1-6 As a prisoner bound to the Master, I call on you to conduct yourselves in a manner that befits the summons you have received. Live among yourselves in love for one another with complete humility and genuine courtesy, patiently bearing with one another. I call on you to do your part to maintain the unity of the spirit that brings you together in harmony. You are called together into one body and in one spirit by the very fact that God's call unites you in one hope. We have one Master, one allegiance, one commitment. We have the one God, the Father of all of us, who is ruler over all of us and who creates through all of us and is present among all of us.

4:7-16 To each one of us has been given a share of God's

gracious goodwill as his part of the gift of Christ. For we are told: "He has gone up to the height.

He has caught his captives.

He has given gifts to men."

But what does it mean: "He went up," if not that he had already gone down into the heart of our world? The very one who went down, went up to fill the universe with his presence. He himself gave the appointments: some to be his official messengers, some to be spokesmen for him, others to proclaim his good news, and others to watch over and teach us. These appointments were given so as to fit God's people for the work of service—for their conduct of his church: "the body of Christ." So shall we all at last arrive at the unity inherent in our faith in, and in our knowledge of, the son of God. So shall we all at last reach a maturity measured by the completeness of Christ. Then we will no longer be babies, agitated, unsteadied, by every pressure of propaganda which tricky and crafty men use to confuse the people. Maintaining truth with love we shall in everything grow toward him who is the head —Christ himself. It is from the head [Christ] that the whole body [the church] is joined together, knit together, by the joints and ligaments with which it is provided. The body grows as each individual part functions according to its capacity, and builds itself up in love.

4:17-24 Now, this Christ is our master, I tell you, and, as from him, I charge you: conduct your lives no longer as do people of the world. They live off-center, their minds fixed on futile things. Their minds and hearts are disposed to shady things. They are strangers to the life of God. They are ignorant among themselves through their hearts' insensitivity. They have become callous. They have abandoned themselves to sensual living, to impure habits, and to every kind of disregard for the rights of others. But it is different with you. You have acquired Christ as a habit of life; you have, that is, if you are attentive to him and are disciplined by him, by the reality of meaning found in Jesus. Christ taught you to throw off your old way of life. It was spoiling—all mixed up by your lusts. But now you are to be daily made new in your mental attitude.

Be the new person God created you to be, living an upright life, a life of wholesome integrity and responsibility to God.

4:25-29 Having stripped falseness away then, speak truth each with the next man, because we belong to one another as the parts of one body. Be indignant at wrongdoing, and do not do wrong yourself. Do not let any day come to an end with you still fuming in exasperation. Don't give the devil a chance at you. Any one of you for whom pilfering has been a habit must no longer take anything not his. Instead, he should work hard, engage himself in useful work with his own hands so that he has enough to share with those in need. Don't let any foul language come out of your mouths. But do speak the good word that is suitable for the occasion—helpful words to others, words that build the morale and the spirit of the church.

4:30-32 Also, be careful not to cross God's guiding spirit, his presence among you. His spirit has marked you as the people who belong to God's future, to the time when all will be restored to him and you will be fully free in him. Now that you are a new people of God, let there be no trace of bitterness or of any strong passion or anger, or of any clamor and insults or of any kind of ill will. Rather, be kind to one another, tenderhearted, forgiving, as God in Christ forgives you.

5:1-2 As children, then, secure in their father's love, become God's imitators. Lead loving lives in the way Christ loved you and completely gave himself for you. This is the good way to worship God.

5:3-14 And because you are God's consecrated people it is right that among you there should not be even a suggestion of sexual promiscuity, of dirty words of any kind, or any greedy disregard for the rights of others. Nor should there be any indecency, inane or facetious talk among you. That is in bad taste. Instead, your conversation should be in a mood of gratefulness. For you can be sure of this: no one who is sexually promiscuous or filthy-minded, or who takes advantage of others to gratify himself (all these are ways of setting oneself in the place of God) has any part in the inheritance of

God's and Christ's community. Do not let anyone deceive you with shallow theories. These are the practices of those who ignore God and thereby incur the anger of God. So do not become caught up in their doings. Your lives were once as dark as darkness, but now, in your Master's company your lives are as light as the light. So conduct yourselves as enlightened people. Enlightenment shows itself in wholehearted goodness, rightness, trueness. Make sure what it is that squares with God. Quit associating yourselves with useless activities of a shady character. Instead, expose them. For it is degrading even to talk about the things that go on among them secretly. But everything which is exposed to the light is clearly seen for what it is, and what is clearly seen is reflection of the light.

There is a saying about this:

"Wake up, sleeper,
And rise up from among the dead,
And Christ will shine upon you."

5:15-18 See to it, then, that your lives are disciplined, as people sensible to value, not senseless. Make the most of your time, for these are difficult days. So don't be frantic. Be intelligent about what is the will of God. Don't go drowning yourself in drink. Do not dissipate. Be alive!

5:19-21 Talk among yourselves, using psalms and hymns, and song; and make music to God with all your hearts. Be thankful to God (who is our Father) always and for everything with the gratitude of our master, Jesus Christ. In awe of Christ, subordinate yourselves to one another.

5:22-24 Wives, live for your own husbands, as you live for God. The husband should be of first importance to the wife, as Christ should be of first importance to the church. It is he who keeps the church alive as his body. But as the church lives for Christ, so should the wife live for her husband in every way.

5:25-33 Husbands, love your wives the way Christ has loved the church. He gave himself for it. Christ gave himself for the church to make it God's people when they had confessed their faith in him—in the act of baptism—and made a clean break with their past. Christ did this to place the church beside him in splendor, with no spot or flaw, or any other unsightliness. Christ has given the church its special significance and has made it blameless. This is the way husbands should love their own wives—with the same solicitude they have for their own bodies. It could be said that he who loves his wife thereby loves his body. For no one is against his own physical well-being. On the contrary, he promotes his health and strength; he takes care of it, just as Christ does his church, which is *his* body; and we are the limbs of his body.

"Therefore, a man shall leave his father and mother
And shall attach himself to his wife; and the two shall become one."

This is profoundly significant! But *I* am taking this as a symbol of the relationship between Christ and the church. Nevertheless, this also applies to *you,* as individuals. Every husband among you must love his wife as himself. And let the wife look up to her husband.

6:1-3 Children, obey your parents. It is right that you should. Honor your father and mother. That is the first rule that contains a promise. The promise is: "that you may prosper and have long life on earth."

6:4 You, fathers, do not provoke your children to resentment. But educate them in an awareness of God and direct their minds to the meaning of God.

6:5-9 Employees, be responsible to your employers—in matters pertaining to your employment—with respectfulness and humility. Do your work with as much sincere dedication as you would give to Christ. Do not work merely when under the employer's eyes, or only with an eye to human recognition. Consider yourselves workers for Christ, conscientiously doing God's will. Put your service to good purpose for God, not for men. For you can be sure that each of us, whatever his status in man's social scale, is repaid by God for good workmanship. As for you who superintend the work of others, you must show them the same integrity you expect of them. Do not be harsh. For you know very well that both they and you have the same Supreme Employer and he has no favorites.

6:10-17 From now on, all of you, be powered by God, vigorous in the vitality that comes from him. Get into the battle equipment God gives you so that you may be able to stand up to the stratagems of his adversary. Our struggle is not against human enemies. It is against dehumanizing threats to our personhood, against standardization, against the pressures of feverish activity in a universe that seems empty of sense, a struggle for ultimate meaning against forces of futility. This is the reason you need to get into the battle dress God provides you. Then you will be able to keep your balance in time of crisis and, having subdued all adversity, to keep your stability. So stand your ground, with firm conviction, prepared to strike, wearing integrity like a bulletproof vest. Have your communications system in readiness to send out the good news of peace. Especially take up the shield of commitment to God. With this you will be able to put out all the flaming missiles of the enemy. And put on the helmet he gives you (he who makes your life secure with him). And take the weapon his spirit gives you—God's orders.

6:18-20 Be continually in prayer, referring everything to God. Keep your mind on him all the time. Be alert about it. Persist in it, and be in prayer for all God's people. And pray for me that the right words may come to my mind when I open my mouth to speak, that I may boldly, freely, and clearly communicate the meaning of God's purpose. (For this I am an ambassador—in custody.) Pray that when I tell it, I may speak freely as it is necessary for me to speak.

6:21-22 I am sending this letter with Tychicus. He is one of us in God's family—a dependable worker, loyal to the Master. Because you also are interested in knowing how things are with me, he will tell you everything I am doing. That is why I am sending him to you—to let you know all about us and to draw us closer together.

6:23-24 Best wishes to you, my brothers; may peace be yours and may you have the love with integrity that comes from God our Father, and from the master, Jesus Christ. May the graciousness of God's love be among all of you who love our master, Jesus Christ. *For Ever.*

NOTES

EPHESIANS 1

1. George Croly, "Spirit of God."
2. *Westminster Shorter Catechism.*
3. Edgar S. Brightman, *Religious Values* (New York: Abingdon Press, 1925), p. 76.
4. Emil Brunner, *The Divine Imperative,* trans. by Olive Wyon (Philadelphia: Westminster Press, 1947), p. 199.
5. Friedrich Nietzsche, *Thus Spake Zarathustra,* trans. by Thomas Common, I, xi.
6. "Be Thou My Vision," *The Poem Book of the Gael,* trans. by Eleanor Hull. Used by permission of Chatto & Windus, Ltd., publishers.
7. Lesslie Newbigin, "The Summons to Christian Mission To-day," *The International Review of Missions,* XLVIII (1959), 185.
8. T. W. Manson, *The Servant-Messiah* (New York: Cambridge University Press, 1953), p. 98.
9. *Ibid.*

EPHESIANS 2

1. C. F. Andrews, *Christ in the Silence* (London: Hodder & Stoughton, 1933), p. 92.
2. Brunner, *The Divine Imperative,* p. 55.
3. T. S. Eliot, *Murder in the Cathedral.* Used by permission of Harcourt, Brace & World and Faber and Faber Ltd.
4. Hendrick Kraemer, *The Communication of the Christian Faith* (Philadelphia: Westminster Press, 1956), p. 10.
5. Samuel Taylor Coleridge, "The Rime of the Ancient Mariner."

EPHESIANS 3

1. C. S. Lewis, *The Great Divorce* (New York: The Macmillan Company, 1946), p. 58.

2. George Matheson, "Make Me a Captive, Lord."
3. Claude G. Montefiore, *The Old Testament and After* (New York: The Macmillan Company, 1923), p. 211.
4. Croly, "Spirit of God."
5. William Wordsworth, "Lines Composed a Few Miles Above Tintern Abbey."
6. Georgia Harkness, *Understanding the Christian Faith* (Apex ed.; Nashville: Abingdon Press, 1947), pp. 12-13.
7. William Shakespeare, *The Merchant of Venice.*
8. Louis Fischer, *The God That Failed,* ed. Richard Crossman (New York: Harper & Row, 1949), p. 225.
9. Abraham Joshua Heschel, *God in Search of Man* (New York: Farrar, Straus & Cudahy, 1955), p. 281.
10. Sydney Cave, *Redemption, Hindu and Christian* (London: Oxford University Press, 1919), p. 194.
11. Nietzsche, *Thus Spake Zarathustra,* II, xxxix.

EPHESIANS 4

1. Erich Fromm, *The Art of Loving* (New York: Harper & Row, 1956), p. 120.
2. Rudyard Kipling, "Non Nobis Domine."
3. Heschel, *God in Search of Man,* p. 154.
4. John Greenleaf Whittier, "We May Not Climb the Heavenly Steeps."
5. Laurence Housman, "Brother Sun," *Little Plays of St. Francis* (London: Sidgwick & Jackson, Ltd., 1952), II, 90.
6. Eliza Scudder, "The Quest."
7. Frances R. Havergal, "Lord, Speak to Me That I May Speak."
8. *Ibid.*
9. Frances R. Havergal, "Take My Life and Let It Be."
10. Henry Wadsworth Longfellow, "A Psalm of Life."
11. John Greenleaf Whittier, "Dear Lord and Father of Mankind."

EPHESIANS 5

1. C. S. Lewis, *Mere Christianity* (New York: The Macmillan Company, 1952), p. 128.
2. Euripides in "Phoemissoe," *Fragments.*
3. John Keble, "Sun of My Soul."
4. Mozarabic Liturgy (seventh century).
5. "God Moves in a Mysterious Way."
6. William Shakespeare, *Antony and Cleopatra,* II, vii.
7. Harry Emerson Fosdick, "God of Grace and God of Glory." Used by permission of Harry Emerson Fosdick.
8. Henry van Dyke, "Joyful, Joyful, We Adore Thee." Used by permission of Charles Scribner's Sons.
9. *Ibid.*
10. *Ibid.*
11. Robert Browning, "Any Wife to Any Husband."

EPHESIANS 6

1. Whittier, "Dear Lord and Father of Mankind."
2. Lecomte du Noüy, *Human Destiny* (New York: David McKay Co., 1947), p. 225.
3. Havergal, "Lord, Speak to Me That I May Speak."